ALL IT'S

TO BE

Bryan Clark

BACK TO THE BIBLE
Publishing

ALL IT'S MEANT TO BE
© 2000 by Bryan Clark

BACK TO THE BIBLE PUBLISHING
P.O. Box 82808
Lincoln, Nebraska 68501

Editor: Anne Severance
Cover design: Robert Greuter & Associates
Cover illustration: PHOTODISC, Inc.
Interior design: Laura Poe
Art and editorial direction: Kim Johnson

Additional copies of this book are available from Back to the Bible Publishing. You may order by calling **1-800-759-2425** or through our Web site at **www.resources.backtothebible.org**.

1 2 3 4 5 6 7 8 9 10 – 05 04 03 02 01 00

ISBN 0-8474-0713-6

Printed in USA

Dedication

To Patti, my "one-flesh" partner. She fills each day with joy and cultivates within me a longing for an ever more intimate relationship with God. We have journeyed together to understand our sexuality before God that we might experience all it's meant to be. I love you!

Acknowledgments

With grateful appreciation to Warren Wiersbe, who has been my friend and encourager. He challenged me to put this material in print.

Thanks to Tom Schindler and Kim Johnson at Back to the Bible, who worked so hard and so well to make this book the best it could be.

Thanks to Mags, Robin, and Greg for their part in the creative process.

Thanks to Anne Severance, who not only took the manuscript and made it better, but also was a delightful encourager along the way.

Thanks, everyone!

Contents

Introduction 11

Parable of the King's Feast..13

1. Passion—or Pain? 19

2. Welcome to the Real World 23

3. Why Settle for Less When God Wants You to Have More? 29

Parable of the Father's Photo 37

4. Image Is Everything 41

5. No More Lonely Nights 47

6. Empty Promises, Empty Lives 55

7. Could You Be Guilty of Sexual Idolatry? 63

8. Why Sex Was Never Meant to Be a Hit-and-Run 69

Parable of the Dancing Puppet 77

9. When Satan Pulls the Strings 83

10. Pleasure with a Price Tag 91

11. How to Have Lasting Sexual Fulfillment 101

Parable of the Gardener and the Flower 109

12. Midnight in the Garden 115

13. For Singles Only: How Far Is Too Far? 123

14. Amazing Grace—God Really Does Forgive 129

15. The Road to Paradise 137

Parable of the Golden Goblets 145

Foreword

We get mail! As four gals on the go, we have the privilege—and pain—of meeting and hearing from a lot of fans who are willing to share their hearts. As a result, we know some of the stuff that's going on out there, from Small Town, USA, to the lights and lure of the big cities. We do more than sing for a living. We listen—and we care. That's why we were so excited to find a book that addresses many of the issues we read about in our fan mail.

The struggle with temptation is not new. What is new is the style in which Pastor Bryan Clark retells the old, old stories—and a few new ones—with a surprising twist. He reminds us that when our first parents, Adam and Eve, fell into temptation, they brought down the whole human race. Today, with our inherited sin nature and ever-increasing access to the dark side of the secular media, much that looks really good on the outside is constantly in our face. "Taste this," we are told, "and you'll be satisfied."

But Christians don't have to buy into the world's view of what brings joy and happiness. We don't have to use trial and error, take a wild guess, or follow the pack. We have the real Answer Book. In the Bible is every possible scenario for living—with the way to happiness built in. Pastor Clark says it's easy: The path to avoiding sexual temptation is by renewing our minds through the rock-solid principles found in the Scriptures. Unless we actively saturate ourselves with what God says about the subject, we will not be vulnerable to all that the world is throwing at us.

There are plenty of books on sexuality, but this one is unique in its simplicity. Rather than fearing ridicule by waiting until marriage to have sex, you can be empowered, inspired, and challenged to live a life of holiness. Obviously, waiting is not for wimps. It takes courage and determination. But Pastor Clark shows you why it's worth the wait. Since God created sex in the first place, He ought to know best how it works to bring ultimate fulfillment.

Developing a "theology of sexuality" will give you a head start on true happiness. This book is not about having less sex. It's about discovering how to have more—of all it's meant to be!

—Heather, Denise, Shelley, and Terry
POINT OF GRACE

Introduction

Once upon a time… Ah, these words transport us into lands unknown. They escort us to a realm where knights in shining armor rescue beautiful maidens from fire-breathing dragons. They take us across the seven seas to adventures untold. These simple words invite us to that place where people live happily ever after. I find within my heart a longing for such a place.

This morning I was up until 2:00 A.M. sitting by the bedside of a dear saint dying of cancer. As his family looked on, he quietly passed away. Absent from the body, present with the Lord. I have seen death many times, but I continue to marvel at its meaning. One moment a person is struggling to stay alive on this earth, and the next he is more alive than he's ever been—in the presence of God. Maybe that's why my heart resonates with the words *once upon a time*. There really is such a place and time. A place with no sorrow. A place with no pain. A place with no more partings. It's a place prepared by God for His beloved.

I also find that there was such a place in the beginning. As I open my Bible, I'm not even two pages into it before I discover a garden paradise called Eden. The Bible not only describes it as a place where the fruit was good to eat, but also a place that was pleasurable to the eyes. It was what we would call a fantasyland. A once-upon-a-time kind of place. Something deep in my soul yearns to walk with God in such a garden—to know this kind of intimacy and pleasure.

All It's Meant to Be seeks to take you there—out of the cold, damp dungeon of our culture and into a delicious garden of delight.

Have you ever wondered where pleasure comes from? Many people are convinced that God wants us to experience less pleasure than the world has to offer. Is that true? If so, then why did God create us as pleasure-seeking beings in the first place? Or set His first creations in a garden of unparalleled beauty, appealing to all the senses? Why did He create sex? Could there be more to this sexuality thing than can be discovered through trial and error?

In the '70s people were promised a life of sexual satisfaction if they would only cast off the restraints and experience sexual freedom. Are we more satisfied now—thirty years after our so-called sexual liberation—than then? The evidence supports the opposite conclusion. People today are more frustrated and unfulfilled sexually than ever before. Our culture is sex-crazed because sex is not satisfying. Like the proverbial dangling carrot, ever promising delight, yet never permitting the consummation of pleasure.

Something is clearly wrong. What can we do about it?

This book will take you on a journey to discover how your God-given sexuality can lead you to pleasure forevermore. You will learn why the Creator designed us the way He did. Why He made us with such strong sexual drives and how to satisfy these passions in a way that is honorable and pleasing to Him. Married couples and singles alike will discover the recipe for a taste of the paradise God created in the beginning and the Paradise that is awaiting His children on the other side of death.

These pages offer both hard-hitting truth about sex as well as an occasional escape into fantasyland through a series of parables, scattered throughout the book. The parables—Jesus' favorite method of truth-telling—will encourage you to dream a little, while the instructional chapters will show you how to turn those dreams into reality.

I trust that you will settle for nothing less than to experience all He has lovingly prepared for you in the area of your sexuality—all it's meant to be.

Parable of
the King's Feast

✝

Parable of the King's Feast
†

There once was a king who ruled his kingdom with a firm hand and a loving heart. Over and over through the years, he had demonstrated care and compassion for his people.

As if this were not enough, he sent out an invitation to everyone in a nearby village to attend a royal feast. The king promised that this would be a feast unlike any other.

On the day of the feast, an air of excitement and anticipation hummed through the streets as the villagers tried to imagine what rare treats might be included on the menu. These poor villagers had existed on simple fare most of their lives and were unaccustomed to the delicacies reserved for royalty. But today they would dine at the king's table!

When everyone arrived outside the castle gates, they were greeted by a servant, escorted inside and led to a large room. Around the perimeter of the room were tables covered with cloths. The servant explained that the king had given strict orders that the village people were to wait here for their audience with the king. They were not to eat or even to taste any of the food until the appointed hour.

For a while the people waited patiently, but their patience wore thin as empty bellies began to rumble. Some wondered if the king might be toying with them for his own amusement. All agreed that their hunger pangs made the waiting difficult, and wished the king would call for the feast to begin.

Lured by tantalizing aromas, someone, more out of curiosity than mischief, pulled back one of the cloths and found a tempting array of edibles such as the villagers had never seen. Soon all the cloths were yanked off the tables, and great mounds of food beckoned to be tried and tasted.

Some of the villagers reminded the others of the king's instructions. But most of them were soon persuaded to indulge themselves—and indulge they did. They crammed their mouths full of everything they could get their hands on. "What a feast!" they cried as they stuffed themselves in their gluttony.

A small group of obedient subjects refused to participate in the eating frenzy, choosing instead to obey the king's orders. But when the food was all but consumed, even these began to wonder if they had missed out on the feast altogether.

Then, just as their neighbors were finishing up the last crumbs, a large wooden door swung open, and a trumpet fanfare announced the arrival of the king.

A tense silence charged the atmosphere as the king's gaze swept the room, taking in the empty tables and full bellies. Some of the guilty villagers cowered, fearing the king's wrath. Others whispered defiantly, "Well, what did he expect? It wasn't our fault we were hungry, and he was nowhere to be found!"

But not one of them was prepared for what followed. There was no anger on the king's countenance, no condemnation—only disappointment. "What have you done?" he asked softly. "This was food we had discarded and were preparing to feed the livestock. These stale leftovers were not the feast I intended for you."

The villagers stared at one another in confusion and dismay. Finally one of them spoke up. "O King, we were so hungry! We thought this was the feast you had promised. We could not wait any longer!"

"Yes, you could have waited," replied the king, "but you chose not to. You have filled yourselves with leftovers, and now you are too full to enjoy the feast I had prepared for you."

Then, catching the king's eye was the small group of faithful subjects who had followed his orders and refused to eat the forbidden food. "Come," he called to them. "Enter the banquet room and feast to your heart's content. Because you have listened to my voice, you will experience a feast the others can now only dream of."

To those with crumbs still on their mouths, he said, shaking his head sadly, "You did not trust me, so you did not obey me. And now you must be satisfied with the choice you have made."

With that, weeping and mourning over what they had lost by their impetuous actions, the foolish villagers were shown out of the king's presence. But there was no way to undo what had been done. They would miss the feast.

Meanwhile, the king celebrated with those who had chosen to abide by his wishes. "It was hard to wait," admitted one loyal follower, "especially when everyone else was eating. But we knew that the only way to

16

enjoy the king's feast was to obey."

"Yes," he said, "that is true. But I ask you: Why settle for food fit only for animals when I have provided a feast fit for a king?"

Chapter 1
Passion—or Pain?

Sex! All we have to do is mention the word and folks begin to squirm.

Some gasp, "You're writing a book on *what?*" A few—even in this era of sexual sophistication—still blush. Others hide their discomfort by speaking in crusty terms. There are even the self-proclaimed experts who want us to believe they've got this sexuality thing wired. Yet, when it's all said and done, there is a lot of confusion surrounding the subject of sex.

Take, for example, an ABC *Prime Time Live* special that aired on March 20, 1996, entitled, "Sex, Truth, and Videotape." The segment featured teenagers interviewing their peers. At first, the kids were laughing and hamming it up for the cameras, but their discomfort was obvious. They wanted to give the impression they had it all together, that they were sexually active and having a great time!

As the cameras continued to roll, however, we got a peek behind the masks. It soon became clear that for many, sexual activity had created more pain than passion. A fire that warms is also a fire that burns.

One girl shared honestly from her heart. "I was thirteen and it was my best friend's brother and I — I barely remember it. But what I do remember is that it was one of the worst experiences of my whole life!" Another girl confessed, "I was with a guy in a — someone's party and he was my boyfriend for five months and then — then we had sex, but it didn't really work, so he went out of the room and left me there naked. And I was sitting there crying."

Still another put it this way. "To a girl, it's like losing your childhood. I mean, I felt like I wasn't a little girl anymore and it really hurt. You know, I wanted to be little again. And sometimes, like — sometimes, like I say, I had sex during the day, and then I'd go home and I'd sit there and want to be a little girl so bad, and it would just make me feel so horrible and, like—so dirty."

Things weren't very funny anymore. Confidence no longer oozed from those on camera. Once we got a good look at the real people, what we saw was a lot of pain.

After the giggling and coarse language stops, what we find are people being destroyed because they underestimate the power of sexuality. Our culture is full of lonely people who huddle around a fire to experience warmth, only to come away with serious burns. Sex can be a powerful expression of love, but it also can be a powerful tool for destruction. Like gasoline, if not used properly, sex can leave lifelong scars.

Hollywood's Lie

Angie looked across the dance floor, scanning the room to see who was there. The eyes of half the guys on the dance floor met hers as her glance swept by. She was one of the most attractive and sought-after girls in school. Most of the guys would have gladly left their dates that night if they could have had Angie. But she was used to that. She passed by the guys that night like they were generic cola on sale.

Then it happened. The quarterback from the local college stepped into the gym. He was every girl's dream. While most of the guys were checking Angie out, most of their dates had their eyes riveted on Luke.

What happened in the next thirty minutes has been scripted for a thousand B movies. Luke danced with a few lucky girls and Angie danced with a few lucky guys. Then, Luke's eyes met Angie's, and they knew the next dance was theirs.

Almost as mysteriously as he had arrived, Luke disappeared—only this time he was not alone. Luke and Angie spent the night together in his parents' cabin on the lake. The fire glowed in the background as the two responded to each other as if they'd written the book on making love. It was paradise.

A couple of days later they met to talk. Both were all smiles and dressed to kill. "What we shared was beautiful," Luke said warmly. "I'll always remember our night together, but I'm not ready for a relationship." Angie didn't miss a beat. "Oh, I didn't expect a commitment," she tossed off a casual reply. "What we had together was special, and I will always love you for that. But I have my own plans."

Luke lifted a brow. "Maybe another time then? For old time's sake?"

"Sure. Call me." Angie's smile is bright, her voice, dripping with honey. With that, the two go their separate ways, more fulfilled and more complete, having experienced one glorious night of passion.

What Hollywood communicates about sex is a myth that could have devastating consequences to those who buy it.

Reality Check

Hollywood fills the airwaves with this kind of subtle deception by the hour. Big-time producers are determined to convince you that what you see on the screen is for real. They want you to believe that sex is the route to fulfillment and meaning in life. That couples can experience one-night stands like Luke and Angie's with no physical or emotional consequences. What these writers of fiction communicate about sex is a myth that could have devastating consequences to anyone who buys it.

Have you ever considered the fact that most of Hollywood is made up of writers, directors, and actors who don't have a clue about how to make a relationship work? Many of those who pretend to have it together in the movies change partners in real life as often as they change their socks. What could they possibly know about intimacy, love, and sex?

Is it possible that some of these people live out their fantasies on screen to escape the real world? Is there any evidence to prove they know what they're talking about? Isn't it something like a person who has lost his arms and legs working with explosives and claiming to be able to instruct you on how to handle TNT? Why would you want to take his advice? He doesn't have a leg to stand on!

Real life, as viewed at the box office, isn't real life at all. It's a fantasyland. Yet many try to imitate what they see in the movies. They hope to find something as beautiful when they return to their not-so-beautiful world outside the theater. Never forget, though, that when the director yells, "Cut!" and the scene ends, these actors leave the set, many to return to fractured and dysfunctional relationships.

In real life, sexuality doesn't work like it does in the movies. We keep hoping and praying and wishing on a star that things will be different. But when the house lights go up, the movie's over.

I drive by the junior high school and see plenty of young people confused about sexuality. You can spot it in the way they dress and the way they act around members of the opposite sex. How many potential friendships are lost because a boy and girl can't relate to each other without sexual interference?

I see men in midlife playing the fool in a desperate attempt to satisfy the longing of an empty soul. People looking for love and romance on the Internet because they can no longer bear the pain of personal rejection. Aching hearts. A rash of insecurity. We've now reached a point in our culture when we are encouraged to flaunt our stupidity as a badge of honor. Sexual idiots make entertaining guests on talk shows.

Sex is no longer defined as a meaningful experience between two people in love. Sex is something to get. Sex is raw and tough. Sex is selfish to the core. A challenge to be conquered. A rite of passage. It's fodder for dirty jokes and perverse conversations. Any thoughts of sex being anything more than a selfish attempt to go for the gusto are buried beneath layers of lust and disappointment.

In Your Dreams

Wouldn't it be great if you could wake up in Wonderland, where every love story had a happy ending? Where there were no divorce statistics, no STDs, no lying or cheating or sleeping around on other people's spouses?

In my *dreams*! you say. I should *be* so lucky!

Well, what if there were a way to find perfect love and fulfillment? To experience sexuality and pleasure to the highest degree possible? Wouldn't it be worth a little time, a little effort, a little prayer if you could find someone who could answer your deepest need for fulfillment? If so, you've come to the right place.

Oh, we may not have all the answers, but we know where to send you for help. And we wouldn't want you to end up like Angie . . . .

Chapter 2
Welcome to the Real World

Angie is a fictitious character, but her story is true. In fact, it is a compilation of dozens of stories.

This young woman had it all together. She was sharp, funny, and full of dreams. She made good grades at school, was on the student council, played volleyball, and ran track. She was kind and loving and very popular with her fellow students. Angie never had to worry about getting a date. She was pretty and carried herself with a certain kind of confidence that made her attractive to the guys at school. Yeah, Angie had it all together.

Back home, though, things weren't so together. Angie's mom and dad divorced when she was in grade school. Her father was verbally abusive. Angie and her two sisters were sad about the divorce, but relieved to be rid of the abuse.

As the oldest, a lot of the responsibility fell on Angie's shoulders. What others saw as confidence was more likely the result of having to grow up too soon. Angie's mom did the best she could, but being a single parent wasn't easy.

All her life Angie had longed to be special to her dad.

On the surface anyway, Angie seemed to be handling things well. She was pleasant and fun to be around. She carried some anger toward her father and occasionally directed it toward other guys. "Men are all alike," she would sometimes mutter to her mom. No matter what her mother said about giving guys a chance, Angie's mind was made up.

Then Angie met Steve. Steve was everything her father was not—kind, compassionate, and ready to listen to everything Angie had to say. All her life Angie had longed to be special to her dad. She had longed to sit on his lap and have him tell her stories or read to her. She had longed to go on walks with him and talk about her hopes and dreams. Her heart cried out for a daddy who would be proud of his little girl . . . but it never happened.

Angie's mom had gotten pregnant when she was in high school and married Angie's dad. Both would admit they were never in love—just trying to make the best of a bad situation. Angie's dad once said if they had it to do over again, he would have insisted on an abortion. Now that hurt! Few things he'd ever said had cut as deeply as that comment, and Angie had never forgotten.

Because of her mom's situation, Angie was determined not to make the same mistake. She attended a local church youth group and was committed to waiting until marriage before becoming sexually involved. At first it seemed easy to resist temptation. After all, if most of the guys were like her dad . . . .

When Steve came along, he pushed all the right buttons. Steve was the first guy who made Angie feel special. The first guy to give her what she had needed from her dad. Steve generated feelings in Angie that she had never felt before. Like desirable. Like important. Like somebody really cared. She was even beginning to feel safe and protected.

Once in awhile, Steve attended youth meetings with Angie, but he didn't seem very comfortable there. Oh, he believed in God and was "religious" in his own way. He often told Angie how much he respected her high moral values. He even agreed with them. But Steve was getting pressure from his buddies at school. Most of them were sexually active and were giving Steve grief for not going all the way with Angie. At first he laughed it off, but over time, the pressure to impress his friends became more intense.

Angie was still determined to maintain her purity, but she knew deep in her heart this relationship was different. Resisting Steve's advances was getting harder to do. The last thing she wanted was to upset Steve or drive him away. In fact, she was terrified of losing him and would do almost anything to keep him happy.

She knew that, like a runaway train, he would not stop this time.

Runaway Emotions

One Saturday Angie's dad came by the house for a visit. At first things were pleasant enough. Angie had learned to maintain emotional distance from her dad to avoid getting hurt. Her sister, on the other hand, didn't beat around the bush and said what she thought. As usual, a shouting match exploded between Angie's sister and her dad. Pretty soon everyone was involved, and her dad said a few choice things about all of them and stormed out of the house.

Angie needed to escape the pain of yet another round with her dad, so she ran to Steve. When he held her, the world seemed to stop. She could hide in his arms, like a child climbing into Mommy's lap. Exactly what happened after that, she is not quite sure to this day.

All she can remember is that she was angry with her father and needed Steve's protection. The closer he held her, the safer she felt. And Steve, probably sensing her vulnerability at this moment, decided to take advantage of it. It was pretty clear he was in no mood to turn back now.

Angie had an idea where things were headed. She knew Steve had wanted to go all the way for some time now. Like a runaway train, he would not be able to stop this time. Sure, her head knew she should slow things down, but her heart could not bear the thought of making Steve angry with her and possibly rejecting her. She felt so safe, so loved, so desirable. It had to be right. That day they had sex together for the first time.

Immediately afterward, things were pretty awkward. Steve didn't say very much. Part of Angie wanted to leave, but where would she go? She certainly didn't want to go home. During the sexual experience, she had felt Steve really loved her and would always be there for her. Now she wasn't so sure. There was a distance between them that she couldn't explain. Things just somehow seemed different.

That night, when she finally did go back home, her emotions were churning. Part of her felt good about what had happened. It was something she'd dreamed about sharing with Steve for several months. In some ways it had been beautiful. In other ways, much to her surprise, she was now feeling things she hadn't expected. She felt empty. She felt lonely, like she'd given away something she couldn't have back. She began to feel sick.

Wrestling with shame and guilt, she didn't sleep at all that night. She knew that what she had done was wrong in the eyes of God. Would He ever forgive her? Would her heavenly Daddy respond like her earthly daddy—in a fit of rage? And what about Steve? Would he expect her to give sexually from now on? What if she didn't? Would he reject her—like her dad? How could something that had started out so great end in such disaster?

Where Will It All End?

In the days that followed, the relationship between Angie and Steve was strained, to say the least. Just as she had feared, Steve expected more sexual involvement, and Angie resisted—at first. But it wasn't long before she gave in.

They slept together several more times, but Angie wasn't into it and Steve could tell. They didn't talk much anymore as sex became the focal point of the relationship. Angie knew she was losing Steve. She was torn between feeling guilty and feeling lost without him.

About the time Angie thought things couldn't get any worse—they did. She learned she was pregnant. She wanted to believe that Steve would be there for her and make the best of the situation, but deep down she was afraid that this would end the relationship. She could see her life shaping up much like her mom's, and her heart sank. What had she done? How could this have happened? She had been so determined to do it right and avoid her mom's problems.

When she told Steve, predictably he erupted. Somehow he made it all seem like it was her fault. He insisted she have an abortion. As a matter of fact, he told Angie that if she didn't abort the baby, he sure didn't plan to stick around and take care of it. This was absolutely the worst-case scenario!

Would she spend the rest of her days alone as a single parent?
Would she ever really know love?

No way would she have an abortion, though. Her convictions were still strong enough that she would not kill her innocent baby. She also knew what that decision meant. She, like her mother, would raise the child as a single parent.

In the next few months, she sat alone at home while her classmates went on with their lives. Complications from the pregnancy made attending school impossible. In many ways it was an easy out. Better to stay home than to face her friends at school every day—especially Steve.

At first, Angie's friends came around to check on her. But after a while, busy with school and other activities, they drifted away. Angie had never felt so alone. No more student council, no more volleyball, no more track, no more parties.

At home all day, she had plenty of time to wonder about the future. Would she finish high school? Would she ever go to college? Would she spend the rest of her days as a single mom? Would she ever really know love?

Today Angie is in her mid-twenties. Her little girl is ten years old and the light of her life. As a matter of fact, little Lisa is about all Angie has. She works for minimum wage. She depends on food stamps and welfare to get her through each month. She dresses in garage sale fashions, and every month she wonders if she will make it. She has no time or energy for a social life. Steve is long gone, as are her friends from high school. The days are exhausting and the nights are long and lonely.

Angie often lies in bed, worn out but unable to sleep. She relives that night with Steve over and over again. She wonders what might have been if she had not had sex with him. Where would she be today? She wonders if she will pay for that mistake the rest of her life. And on those rare occasions when she has time to watch a little TV, she views love— Hollywood style—and scoffs. She believed their lie. She thought it would all turn out the way the movies do.

She picks up the remote, turns off the television, eyes the pile of laundry that still needs to be folded, and mumbles to herself, "Welcome to the real world, Angie."

Chapter 3
Why Settle for Less When God Wants You to Have More?

It seems that everyone is talking about sex these days—from sex scandals to sex idols. The fact that sex is used to advertise everything from perfume to mouthwash, deodorant to cars is not new. Everybody knows that sex sells.

The only thing that's different is the extent to which the media will go—from more obscene to most. Talk show hosts compete to see who can showcase the most bizarre sexual behavior. Recently I saw a commercial for one talk show featuring moms who have sex with their daughters' boyfriends. Another covered teenage girls who only have sex with married men. According to the *Los Angeles Times*, somewhere around sixty colleges across the country today offer courses in "pornology." The curriculum includes watching X-rated movies and striptease dancers, and asks students to create their own pornographic videos.

Sexually active teenagers are searching for fulfillment,

not experiencing it.

Our culture is filled with self-proclaimed "sexperts," claiming that they can help you manage your sex life. What makes them experts? Who gave them their credentials? Even your peers, work associates, and friends, as confused as they are on the subject, don't hesitate to dish out advice.

But remember, experience does not make someone an expert in sexuality any more than watching TV makes someone an expert in electronics. People who are driven to achieve more and more sexual satisfaction reveal their lack of understanding of the meaning and purpose of sex. Could it be that many of those who are most experienced sexually are those who understand it the least? Lack of understanding often drives sexual pursuit.

For example, sexually active teenagers are not having sex because they are so loved and fulfilled in life or because they feel so good about themselves. As a matter of fact, those teens who have a strong sense of love and fulfillment in life are those who are saying no to sex outside of marriage.

It's the teenagers who feel unloved and unfulfilled who tend to be sexually active. They are having sex because they are looking for something they don't have. When the first sexual encounters fail to satisfy, they seek more. They may become the most "experienced," but that doesn't qualify them as experts. They are experienced in the same way a drug addict is experienced. Who needs that kind of expertise?

The sad truth is that sex can't deliver the goods. Sex simply cannot generate love and fulfillment. The momentary thrill quickly passes, leaving people all the more empty and unsatisfied.

Of course, this isn't true of teenagers only. It's true of anyone who is looking for love through sex. Even in a marriage relationship, where God intends for a man and a woman to enjoy sex, it will not satisfy if misused. In marriage, misunderstanding the meaning of sex often leads to deviant behavior—adultery, pornography, or some other substitute.

When it comes to sex, experience is not the best teacher. If sex isn't fulfilling, then more of the same isn't the answer.

What is the real meaning and purpose of sex anyway? Where do we find love and fulfillment? What do we have to do to be satisfied sexually?

One thing seems obvious: Problem drinkers should not give speeches about controlling alcohol consumption. Non-swimmers should not be giving swimming lessons. People who cannot find fulfillment and satisfaction in their own sex lives should not be advising others sexually. So, where do we go for help?

God on Sex? Get Real!

For me, the most disappointing thing about the *Prime Time Live* segment on teen sex was that no real solutions were offered. The host did interview a couple of so-called experts, but they didn't come up with any solid answers.

Several teens poured out the pain created by sexual misuse, but these wounded kids found no lasting hope. Is that really how it is? No hope? No solution? Just an acknowledgment of the pain?

What about those, like Angie, who are now standing on the brink of making choices that could affect the rest of their lives? What do we tell the man tempted to cheat on his wife or the wife about to leave her husband for a friend at work? What do we tell the person enslaved to Internet pornography? What do we tell those who have been wounded so deeply they are afraid to risk loving again?

And what about those who don't want to mess up their lives but are confused by all the hype about sex in our culture? Do we just say, "Tough luck, pal! Better luck next time!"? Who can speak with authority on this potentially destructive subject?

There is one voice that is often missing from discussions on sex. As a matter of fact, it's the only one that counts. He is the expert on human sexuality and can clear the fog. Who is it? God. That's right—God.

"Oh, great! There goes all the fun," some of you are saying to yourselves. "If there is one Person I don't want interfering in my sex life, it's God."

When it comes to sex, God's only concern is not that you will experience too much, but that you will experience too little.

Don't be so sure about that. God has some things to say about sex that may shock you. After all, He is the Creator and Designer of sex. He is the Author of passion and pleasure. If we took all the collective knowledge of every expert in the world on the subject of sexuality and pleasure, it would not equal one drop in God's vast ocean of wisdom. His concern is not that you will experience too much sex, but that you will experience too little. When it comes to sex, God wants you to experience all it's meant to be—and nothing less.

In art class, a teacher will often ask students to interpret a piece of art. What did the artist intend to communicate? What does the work represent? Many can offer opinions, but the only authoritative opinion is that of the artist. Only the artist can say with certainty what he or she was intending to communicate.

What God has to say about sex will allow you to experience sexuality and pleasure to the highest degree.

In the same way, only God can speak with authority on the subject of sexuality. He created it. He designed it. He is the One who should define its purpose and meaning.

Some people seem to think God created sex accidentally, that He somehow stumbled onto it. That God blushes when the subject is mentioned. That "nice" people aren't supposed to enjoy it. Nonsense! Sex is beautiful and holy when used according to the Artist's design. In this sex-crazed culture, God's opinion needs to be taken seriously.

What God has to say about sex will not only clear the confusion, it will allow you to experience sexuality and pleasure to the highest degree. God even dedicated an entire book of the Bible to the beauty of sensual love (see Song of Solomon). It only makes sense that the Author should be consulted on all matters pertaining to sex.

Headlights and Light Bulbs

You cannot take the headlight out of your car and fit it into your reading lamp at home; it just won't work. The headlight was not designed to be a light bulb for the reading lamp. Does this mean that the headlight is useless or that there is something wrong with the reading lamp? Not at all. The headlight was designed for one purpose; the reading lamp, another. When each is used for that which the designer intended, they are both valuable.

When people try to use sex to meet needs it was not designed to meet—such as generating love and fulfillment—they will be disappointed. God has a specific purpose for our sexuality. Used according to His plan, sex is a beautiful and meaningful expression. Used outside of God's plan, it has the potential for disaster. Let's investigate what the original Designer says about the meaning and purpose of sex.

As with most subjects, it is always helpful to go back to the beginning. There are those who believe we are here on this earth by chance. This belief is propagated through the theory of evolution. This theory promotes the idea that through a series of mutations, we have evolved from slime to the sophisticated creatures we are today.

Consistent with that view would be the idea that sexuality is merely a means of reproduction to perpetuate the species. In other words, men and women have sex for the survival of the species. Doesn't sound very romantic, does it? To the evolutionist, sex is nothing more than basic animal instinct, with no more meaning for us than it has for the animal kingdom. Popular movies such as *Basic Instinct* reinforce that belief.

When this view is foremost, the role of society is to control sexual behavior in order to maintain an organized civil society, with little thought given to the moral questions involved. Standards are established around what is and isn't civilized in the opinion of the rule-makers.

Today, sex between any two consenting adults is considered permissible. Many even hold that sex between teenagers is inevitable. And a paper has recently been published in which the authors promote sex between adults and children if the child consents.

None of this should surprise us, given the evolutionary backdrop determining today's morality. As opinions change concerning what is acceptable, so do the moral standards of society. Take homosexuality, for example. While at one time homosexuality was considered unnatural and indecent, it is now promoted as an alternative lifestyle—we are supposedly more "enlightened," aren't we?

Those who question the morality of homosexual behavior are quickly labeled intolerant and judgmental. What's the problem if it doesn't hurt anyone? they argue. (By the way, this is the same argument used to support adults having sex with children!) Who says no one is getting hurt? One doesn't have to look far to find people experiencing deep pain because of consensual sex. I speak with these people on a weekly basis. More importantly, what about the moral questions? What about the design of the Creator? Since when does popular opinion take priority over God's Plan?

The Jungle Out There

Sexual sin is running rampant. Parents, sexually abusing their children. Teachers, making babies with students. The president of the United States, involved with a young intern. Employers, sexually harassing employees. Even ministers have been exposed for having sexual relationships with children. Rape, usually committed by someone known to the victim, is an ever-increasing threat.

The evolutionary beliefs of our culture have reduced sexuality to the level of animals.

As a people, we are acting like animals. When there is no greater code of conduct than the opinion of the majority and no higher motivation for behavior than survival, culture spins out of control. Sexuality becomes nothing more than a meaningless pursuit of self-gratification. Free love produces a lifetime of bondage. Just ask Angie.

The evolutionary beliefs of our culture have reduced sexuality to the level of animals. When describing those who promote such behavior, the Bible says they operate by instinct. "Yet these men [false teachers] speak abusively against whatever they do not understand; and what things they do understand by instinct, like unreasoning animals—these are the very things that destroy them" (Jude 10). Notice what this verse is saying: *Operating by instinct alone will ultimately lead to self-destruction.*

How true. Animal behavior has led to devastation in almost every area of society. From welfare to teen pregnancy, from abortion to sexual abuse, it's become a jungle out there.

Not a Chance

There is another view concerning the source of our existence. According to the Bible, God created all that is and we are part of His grand design. We are not an accident of nature. We are not the product of chance. We are a creation of God.

While many would suggest that belief in a Creator God is the ultimate leap of faith and that evolution is grounded in scientific observation, careful examination of the two ideas reveals just the opposite. Evolution is nothing more than a list of assumptions and guesses, with no basis in fact. Science continues to discover more and more evidence to undermine the credibility of the theory of evolution. In his book *Darwin on Trial*, Philip Johnson exposes the deficiency of the theory. While evolution is passed off as science, the truth is it takes more faith, given the evidence of science, to believe in evolution than in creation.

It must be embarrassing to the evolutionist who continues to find more evidence to support the idea of a Creator God. Creation cannot be proved, of course; an element of faith is always necessary. "By faith we understand that the universe was formed at God's command, so that what is seen was not made out of what was visible" (Heb. 11:3). But there is overwhelming evidence for the idea of a Creator God and much to discredit the other theories.

I'm convinced that every person reading this book
wants to experience love and sex to its fullest extent.
God wants the same thing for you.

The biblical view of a Creator God holds that not only did God create us, but He created our sexuality as well. God created people as male and female to experience something far more glorious than mere survival. What men and women can experience in a sexual relationship, an animal operating according to basic instinct cannot even dream about.

Understanding what God has to say about our sex lives would bring radical and welcomed changes to our culture. The dangerous jungle would become a serene, well-landscaped park. Rather than a place of conquest and survival of the fittest, it would be a place of peace and fulfillment, a place where people experience all God meant sex to be.

Modest Changes . . . Not Enough!

Some studies indicate slight changes in sexual behavior are occurring, but the changes are modest at best. One concern is the fact that these changes are taking place for practical reasons rather than for moral ones. A *Newsweek* poll found 85 percent of those who choose abstinence do so because of a fear of sexually transmitted diseases. Only 40 percent indicated any moral consideration in their choices. In other words, if STDs were no longer an issue, the number of those who would choose abstinence would drop drastically once more.

If your code of conduct runs no deeper than a practical fear of disease or pregnancy, you will not stand strong when the pressure is on. Like Angie, you will give in even though you know you shouldn't. No one wants to mess up his or her life. In fact, I'll go so far as to say I'm convinced that every person reading this book wants to experience love and sex to its fullest extent. Here's good news: God wants the same thing for you. Therefore, the convictions that control your sexual choices must be more deeply rooted than merely fear of disease and pregnancy. Let me put it another way: Your convictions must be stronger than your fear of getting caught!

To win the battle, our choices must be determined by a deeply held conviction reflecting the meaning and purpose of sex and rooted in the very Person of God Himself. To experience all He wants for you, you must learn to view sexuality through His eyes. Together, we will develop a theology of sexuality. When that happens, I guarantee you will never see sexuality in the same way again. Sex will go from a basic instinct to a beautiful expression of love and glorious fulfillment.

You may be surprised to learn that sexuality can teach you a great deal about God Himself. We will discover why God created sex, how it is to be used, and why it can be so destructive if used outside of His plan. We will even discover that some of our most significant beliefs about God are pictured in the sexual relationship.

God has an incredible design for your sexuality. As in the Parable of the King's Feast, why settle for food fit only for animals when God intended for you a feast fit for a king?

Parable of the Father's Photo

Parable of the Father's Photo

†

The old man clung to life like a starving child clings to a scrap of bread. As a wise and loving father, he had spent his days trying to instill in his two sons the secret of living a contented life. Now, he had one last gift to pass on to them before he died.

A man of considerable wealth and power, he was respected by all who knew him. Everyone, including his sons, knew that upon his death his fortune would go to his two boys. Although they loved their father and mourned his inevitable passing, they both spent time dreaming about what they would do with the wealth they would inherit.

The father, knowing his time was at hand, called the boys to his deathbed. He gave each son a small wrapped package with a note attached. The note read: "To my sons whom I love, this is my gift to you. You will receive nothing more and nothing less."

The two sons opened their packages, only to find a photograph of their father dressed in old work clothes, giving each of them a heartfelt embrace. That was all. Just an old photo. When they looked back to their father for an explanation, he was gone.

For a time they simply sat, silent, grieving the loss of their father, bewildered by his gift. As the days passed bewilderment gave way to reality. The boys would receive none of their father's vast assets—only the old photo—as their inheritance. The older son responded angrily by discarding the image of his father, while the younger son, still confused by its purpose, carefully guarded it, determined to discover the meaning of the gift.

Time passed and the two sons journeyed separate paths to make their way in the world. For years the brothers did not communicate with each other. Finally, the younger son received word that his brother was dying and was calling for him.

As the young man arrived, he looked around, impressed by his brother's lavish estate. But he was unprepared for what he found inside. He had expected to see his brother in a sickly condition, but this was not simply physical death. The years had taken their toll, etching lines of pain and dissipation in the gaunt face. The emptiness in his brother's eyes revealed a man whose soul had died long before his body.

Drawing upon his meager reservoir of energy, the older brother told his story. He had spent his life seeking wealth and pleasure. The more he had accumulated, the more he had required. Rather than quenching his thirst, his success had left him thirsty for more.

The dying man stared at his younger brother, who seemed to glow with the light of contentment. "What is the difference between us?" he gasped out. "Was it just meant to be this way?"

"No," replied the younger brother, shaking his head sadly. "You made your choices and I made mine. Those choices determined the paths we have traveled. What made the difference was the image in the photo . . . our father's inheritance to us.

"While you carelessly discarded the photo, I set out to discover why our loving father would leave such a gift. I pondered the photo so often that the image burned itself into my mind. Whenever I had to make significant choices, I remembered that image.

"I remembered Father and all he was about in life. It reminded me that what he had given us money can't buy and pleasure can't equal. Our true wealth was not in gold or silver, but in that image of our father—in what he gave us, in who he was. The picture was to encourage us to be like him. Our father's embrace and all that photo represents was the greatest treasure a man could leave his sons.

"When you discarded the photo, my poor brother, you forgot the image. When you forgot the image, you forgot what really matters, what satisfies. So you spent your life trying to find what you had thrown away."

As the man died, the younger brother remained at his bedside, studying the photograph in his hands. He realized again what a precious treasure he had been given. Were it not for this image, he would have traveled his brother's hopeless path. His father had left him a wealthy man indeed.

Chapter 4
Image Is Everything

When I was in college, I had a friend who owned a painting I really liked. His dad had sent it to him from the Philippines, where his parents were missionaries. Through my friend's family, I was able to buy a similar painting for $15, including shipping charges. What a bargain!

This was no small piece of artwork. The canvas measured about three feet by four feet. However, knowing I'd paid such a small price for the painting caused me to treat it pretty casually.

I hung the picture over my bed in my dorm room. But the cheap frame I had used fell off on a regular basis. The guys on my floor soon learned that if they slammed their fists against the wall in the hallway, the frame would fall off the picture and land on me in bed.

This little ritual became a regular pastime. The guys would slam the wall at all hours of the night and listen to me yell as I dodged the attacking picture frame. Some nights the whole thing would come down, and I would have to scramble free before tossing both the painting and frame across the room to be picked up in the morning. To say the painting was abused would be an understatement.

The key to your sexuality is to view it through the eyes of the God who created you.

Years later I was visiting the friend whose father had sent me the painting, and I commented on the art displayed in his home. He told me that the Philippine artist had become quite popular and our paintings were worth a considerable amount of money.

I had to go dig my painting out of the garage, where it was stored with some other junk. I cleaned it up, put an expensive frame on it, and carefully hung this treasure on the wall of my home. I instructed my kids to be careful when playing in the room because this painting was very valuable. The art I had once abused and tossed off my bed like an old blanket was now a museum piece to be guarded!

What made the difference? It had nothing to do with the painting itself, of course. What changed was my attitude. When I thought the piece of artwork was of little value, I treated it accordingly. When I found out it had great value, my attitude changed, which affected how I treated the painting. No longer was it a junky old thing to abuse. It was a work of art to be protected and cared for properly.

The key to guarding your sexuality is to view it through the eyes of the God who created you. Evolution devalues your worth as a person. It tells you that you are an animal and that your sexuality is nothing but a means of reproduction for the survival of the species. The Book of Genesis, however, reveals a different story. You were created by God, and this has everything to do with how you view your sexuality.

From the Start

A common remedy for evolutionists who can't come up with answers to certain objections is to tack on a few billion years to the equation.

"Hey, Joe, tell me again the scientific formula for how creatures from the ocean became land animals."

"That's easy, Fred. Billions of years!"

"Oh, yeah."

No matter how many billions of years are added to the process, the question is always the same: Why is there something today instead of nothing? How did it all begin? Either there is a Creator who has always been around, or something had to begin from nothing. There are no alternatives.

Since evolutionists deny the idea of an eternal Being, because that Being would have to be God, they wrestle with the question of how something came from nothing. Evolution is a cause-and-effect theory, so they are forced to say that everything started with an effect, which is logically impossible. How does something come from nothing? They talk about self-creation, but that's nonsense. If you don't exist, you can't create yourself. They talk about chance, but chance is merely a mathematical probability, with no ability to cause an effect.

Nope. No matter how you slice it, something or someone had to be in the beginning to cause everything else to be. What is the uncaused cause? God! God was in the beginning. God has always been. God is eternal. God is the only explanation for the origin of life and creation.

There is nothing in the animal kingdom that smacks of romance or relationship.

Genesis states that in the first five days, God created. He spoke into being the heavens and the earth, light and darkness, the sun and moon, water and dry land, plant and trees, fish and birds, and other creatures.

Then God spoke to the animals: "Be fruitful and increase in number" (Gen. 1:28). He designed each kind to reproduce in order to populate the earth. "God made the wild animals according to their kinds, the livestock according to their kinds, and all the creatures that move along the ground according to their kinds. And God saw that it was good" (v. 25).

The animal kingdom functions sexually on the basis of instinct for survival. God created a male and female among the animal kingdom for the purpose of reproduction. Animals don't "fall in love." They don't date around to develop relationships. They don't light candles and put on a CD of "The Hereford Heifers" singing their rendition of "Moooonlight Sonata." There is nothing in the animal kingdom that smacks of romance and relationship. Their sexuality is only the built-in urge to merge.

Sorry to say, many people today see human sexuality in the same way. To these folks, sex is nothing more than a physical act for the purpose of reproduction and self-gratification. Hollywood filmmakers, musicians, and other sex spokespeople have no higher view of sexuality than raw animal instinct.

More Than Animals

However, a dip into Genesis changes all that. After five days of creative activity, God did something radically different. On the sixth day, He made a man and a woman. The divine discussion surrounding their creation is much different from that of the animals. "Then God said, 'Let us make man *in our image*, in our likeness" (1:26a). God made men and women *in His own image*. Nowhere does the Bible claim that animals were created in His image. From the beginning, people were set apart from the animal kingdom.

"Do you mean to tell me that I resemble God in some way?" you may ask. Yes! "You mean I somehow reflect God on this earth?" Yes! Evolution teaches that you are an animal in an impersonal chain of life. Creation teaches that you are a special creation of God, designed to reflect His characteristics on earth. Which do you prefer?

Only a few verses into the Bible, we see that when God created you, He had something special in mind. "Let them [the man and woman] rule over the fish of the sea and the birds of the air, over the livestock, over all the earth, and over all the creatures that move along the ground" (v. 26b). The man and woman were the caretakers of Eden, with dominion over the animal kingdom.

This has a lot to say about those who place a higher value on an animal than on a human life. A tree, a dog, and a person are not of equal value in God's eyes. Only human beings are made in His image.

Are you beginning to get the picture? You are several cuts above the animal kingdom. You're an image-bearer. You are to rule over the animal kingdom. No one has the right to abuse any of God's creation or any of His creatures; with the privilege of dominion over them comes the responsibility of taking care of them.

People who have set no higher value on their sexuality than animal behavior don't realize whom God has created them to be.

In Genesis 2 God gave Adam the responsibility of naming the animals. (The next time you have to spell the word *hippopotamus*, you have Adam to blame!) "Now the LORD God had formed out of the ground all the beasts of the field and all the birds of the air. He brought them to the man to see what he would name them; and whatever the man called each living creature, that was its name. So the man gave names to all the livestock, the birds of the air and all the beasts of the field" (Gen. 2:19–20).

Naming the creatures was a mark of man's authority over the animal kingdom. Naming my kids is a sign of my authority over them, but I don't have the right to name my neighbors' kids or even their pets. That isn't my place.

Kids and Dogs

It is extremely important to where we are going in our study of sexuality to understand how clearly God has distinguished us from the animal kingdom. People who have set no higher value on their sexuality than animal behavior don't realize whom God has created them to be.

When we see ourselves as products of chance on the same level as the animals, we act like animals. Why wouldn't we? What is promoted in our culture as sexual sophistication can be found in any barnyard. Not too impressive.

When God created the animals, He put no moral demands on them. We cannot find one command in Scripture regarding the moral responsibility of animals. Nowhere in the Bible does God try to restrict or control the sexual activity of the animals on moral grounds. They just do what they were programmed by God to do.

I have three children and one dog (and one parakeet and one hamster, if you're interested). I spend a lot of time teaching and training my girls regarding moral choices they must make. I want them to know God's standard and the consequences of ignoring His counsel. My desire is for them to know God personally and to obey Him completely. I want them to fulfill the purpose God has for their lives.

On the other hand, I have never tried to teach my dog a single Bible verse. I do not sit down with my dog and try to teach him to make good moral choices. I don't warn him about the female dogs in the neighborhood and their sly ways. I don't lecture him about hanging out with bad dogs around the block. I don't even make him say please and thank you when he gets a treat.

Is my dog a social misfit? Some may say so, but he's really just a dog. He has no sense of morality. I have trained him to sit and stay and to stop barking like the dog next door (don't get me started on that one!). But I don't discuss with him the implications of his decisions if he chooses to disobey. I just whack him one (nicely, of course) if he doesn't do what he's told.

Why is there such a difference between how I raise my kids and how I raise my dog? I have never (*yet*, but who knows these days?) been accused of prejudice because I don't treat my children and my dog the same. Why? Because common sense dictates that my daughters and my dog are dramatically different creatures.

Just Like Your Father

Part of what it means to be made in the image of God is to have the ability and the responsibility to make moral decisions. You can choose right or wrong, but you are responsible to Him for your choices. God holds you accountable. You can delight in God and obey Him, or you can rebel against Him and walk away. The animals can do neither.

It's obvious that this glorious privilege as image-bearers comes with some serious responsibility. You are not free to roam the "barnyard" without consequences. God has raised you up to experience far more than animal behavior. Your sexuality plays a major role in expressing who you are as God's image-bearer.

Looking at myself and my sexuality through His eyes changes everything. I must learn to value my sexuality the way God values it. I must not settle for animal behavior. I must see His design and purpose for sex.

God does not want to restrict your fun; He wants to celebrate who you are. God doesn't want you to settle for *less*. He wants you to experience *more*—more of what He had in mind when He made you a sexual being, created to represent Him properly to the world. When it comes to sexuality, image is everything. You're a child of the King!

Chapter 5
No More Lonely Nights

The Smiths and the Browns looked on as their children, a boy and a girl, sat watching a video. "Aren't they cute together?" Robin sighed.

"No question about it, they're a match made in heaven," Kim gushed.

"Down, ladies," Robin's husband responded, a bit sarcastically. "They're only six years old!"

You've heard that old phrase, "a match made in heaven." You may have even been the target of some matchmaker's schemes to pair you up. Whether or not God Himself actually puts couples together on earth is for someone else to argue. One thing we do know for sure: Adam and Eve were a match made in heaven.

How Moses, as the writer of Genesis, unveils the creation of Adam and Eve teaches us a lot about what it means to be made in His image. In the last chapter we talked about your ability to make moral choices as a reflection of God's image in you. Another significant facet of the image of God is the ability to be relational. Your ability to be relational with God and with others is unique and further separates you from the animals.

A Dog's Life

I have already introduced you to my dog. Jacob, a golden retriever, is a city dog. Some friends who live in the country have a Labrador retriever named Diamond. Every so often Jacob gets to go out to the country to play with Diamond. They run together, swim in the pond, and tumble in the grass for hours. At first glance, they appear to be the best of friends.

A closer look, however, reveals the fact that they are not really friends at all. They enjoy playing together because that's how dogs are, but they don't really know each other. From the moment they met, they ran and played, but there was no concept of getting acquainted. They didn't do a personality survey. They didn't compare likes and dislikes. They don't think about each other when they are not together. (At least, I don't think they do.) They are just dogs.

While animals may have some sort of relationship with other animals and even with their owners, it is a far cry from the type of relationships people have with each other and with God.

Two's Company

When God recorded the creation of the first man and woman, He placed an emphasis on their ability to be relational. Notice the plural pronouns used for God in Genesis 1:27: "Let *us* make man in *our* image, in *our* likeness." God, as Father, Son, and Holy Spirit, is a relational God. He has lived in community with Himself from eternity past.

You are capable of relationship because of the image of God in you.

In other words, God is one God but three Persons called the Trinity. (If the concept of the Trinity is beyond you, join the club!) The Bible clearly teaches God as Trinity, but we cannot fully grasp all that means. Maybe it's enough right now to know that God understands relationship. He is not distant or unapproachable. He values intimacy and community. And He created you in that mold.

Being relational means you can give and receive love. You can develop intimacy with God and with others. You can communicate and express your feelings for another. You can share your joys and your sorrows.

When God created the animals, He did not refer to Himself in the plural as He did when creating man and woman. He didn't emphasize the relational aspect of His nature. My dog, Jacob, and his "friend" Diamond play, but they don't share their lives. They don't confess their frustration when their masters yell at them for barking too much. They don't express their joy to each other over finding a new bone in the yard. Jacob doesn't sit down with Diamond and try to work through his anger because I've scolded him for chewing up a lawn chair. You'll never hear him say something like, "Diamond, I'm just not sure they love me anymore. Maybe they've found a new pet."

The difference the image makes is obvious, except to Jacob—he thinks he's human!

Boy Meets Girl

Notice the repetition in Genesis 1:27: "God created man in his own image, in the image of God he created him; male and female he created them." Your old ninth-grade English teacher might be tempted to whip out her red pencil. By the end of this verse, you may be thinking, "OK, OK, I get it."

But hold on a minute. These phrases are not saying the same thing at all. The writer is using a Hebrew literary technique to make three significant points in this one verse. The sentence structure gives us a clue.

At the beginning of each phrase is the primary thought the writer wishes to convey. Therefore, the first phrase, "*God created* man in his own image," emphasizes God as Creator. The second phrase, "*in the image of God* he created him," stresses the fact that the first couple was created in God's image. The final phrase of the verse, "*male and female* he created them," introduces the concept of sexuality.

The first man and woman were not just created by God. Not just created in His image. They were created by God, in His image—*male and female*. No other creation of God is presented in this way. Part of how the image of God is expressed in you is in your sexuality. Animals were created male and female for *reproduction only*, but human beings were created male and female for *relationship*. A quantum leap.

Notice what follows these three key phrases. "Be fruitful and increase in number" (v. 28). For those of you who think God wants to ruin your sex life, think again. God's very first command to Adam and Eve was to experience their sexuality—in a place called paradise. Not bad! Right from the beginning, the first couple entered into sexual union as an expression of the image of God.

---

*Of all God's creatures, human beings
are the only ones who relate sexually face-to-face.*

This totally sets us apart from the animal kingdom. Of all the creatures God created, human beings are the only ones who relate sexually face-to-face. All others mate in such a way that relationship is not involved.

We are beginning to see the framework for our sexuality as God intended it. Animals experience the physical act that results in reproduction. People are to experience sexuality in the context of a relationship reflecting the image of God.

Made for Each Other

Genesis 2 clearly emphasizes the beauty of the relationship between Adam and Eve. Some people get confused because the man and woman were created in Genesis 1, then Adam shows up solo in chapter 2. That's because both chapters tell the same story, but from different perspectives. Chapter 1 is like viewing the scene from a vertical vantage point; chapter 2, from a horizontal viewpoint. Chapter 2 emphasizes the importance of the relationship between Adam and Eve. These two were not just ships that passed in the night; they were literally made for each other.

To make His point, God used drama to record the events of the creation of Eve. God certainly could have created both of them at the same time. It wasn't that He forgot to create Eve or didn't know Adam would want a partner. No, God had a plan. From the beginning He knew He would create Eve especially for Adam. The dramatic fashion in which her creation is recorded is to make a point. Adam needed Eve because he was created to be relational, and he was alone.

After all the animals were created, it was pretty obvious that everyone else had a mate, but "for Adam no suitable helper was found" (Gen. 2:20). Right away, God noticed. "It is not good for the man to be alone. I will make a helper suitable for him" (v. 18).

But first, God had all the animals pass by Adam to be named. In the process, maybe Adam was thinking something like this: "My, what a lovely couple the hippos make. And don't the giraffes go neck and neck? And look at the lion couple—they're good together. Hey! How come all these animals have partners except me?"

As many can attest, it is no fun to be traveling single in a doubles' world.

"She Shall Be Called 'Woman'"

Evolutionists and some sociologists would say marriage is a cultural adaptation, providing a means by which two people can live better together than separately. Genesis 2 clearly refutes this notion. God designed Adam and Eve to be together to express relationship.

So God put Adam to sleep and performed the first surgery. He reached into the man to bring forth the woman. As some have said, "From the side nearest his heart." Adam had nothing to do with it; he slept through the whole thing.

When Adam sees Eve for the first time, he can barely contain himself, but our language doesn't do justice to the Hebrew expression. In English, Adam's first words are: "This is now bone of my bones and flesh of my flesh; she shall be called 'woman,' for she was taken out of man" (Gen. 2:23). Sounds something like, "She'll do, I suppose."

That translation is a far cry from the original version. The Hebrew terms are vibrantly alive. More like "Wow!" or "Yippee!" or an emphatic, "Yes!" Suffice it to say that Adam was one happy zookeeper at that moment. He finally had his female counterpart. He had himself a woman, and what a beauty she was! Perfect in every way.

Adam and Eve were created by God *for each other.* While God created animals male and female, their sexuality was no big deal. But when human sexuality is introduced, the fanfare begins! Fireworks explode! Music plays! The . . . OK, you get the picture.

When Adam's and Eve's maleness and femaleness came together in a sexual union, they celebrated the image of God. Unlike the animals, they were created to be capable of loving deeply, sharing their deepest joys and their most profound sorrows, their hopes and dreams.

Sex is connecting at the deepest level of intimacy—an experience that leaves me floundering for words because it defies description. But I know it's true. I feel it in my own "one-flesh" relationship. My wife and I have become one, not only physically, but emotionally and spiritually as well—as if I sometimes can't tell where I end and she begins. As God is intimate with Himself and with those who love and trust Him, so we are created to be intimate with Him and with our one-flesh partner in a way that totally separates us from the animal world.

Sexual Boundaries

Chapter 2 of Genesis ends with a general statement about the boundaries for the human sexual relationship. "For this reason a man will leave his father and mother and be united to his wife, and they will become one flesh" (2:24). Obviously Adam and Eve did not have a mother and father. Here God was merely setting the sexual boundaries for the generations to follow.

Sex apart from relationship is to deny the image of God in us. It's to stoop to animal behavior.

What He was saying is that a man and a woman are to leave their respective homes and be joined. There is no doubt that the phrase "one flesh" refers to a sexual union.

From the very beginning, God established that this "one-flesh" sexual relationship is to be experienced within the context of marriage. While Moses does not use the term *marriage* in Genesis 2:24, this is the bond that is clearly implied and later reinforced in the New Testament. Becoming one flesh means "to cleave together, to be glued together so as not to come apart." In this way marriage is identified as a permanent union, not something to be "entered into lightly," then tossed aside if it doesn't work. The only relationship defined in this way is the marriage relationship. Even the bond between parent and child is eventually broken, with a time of *leaving* home to make the *cleaving* to a mate possible.

Sexuality is not simply a physical act, a way to stimulate your body to feel pleasure. It is an expression of the image of God in you and is to be restricted to a lifelong partner in a marriage relationship. To experience sex outside of God's intended boundary is to ignore the design of the Creator, to reject the image of God, and to drag sexual behavior down to the level of the animals.

"Marriage should be honored by all, and the marriage bed kept pure, for God will judge the adulterer and all the sexually immoral" (Heb. 13:4). So marriage is the only place where sex is *right* before God. In fact, He *encourages* it—with the right person, in the right place, at the right time!

Naked and Shameless

The final verse of chapter 2 offers a beautiful description of the sexual relationship. Adam and Eve were both "naked, and they felt no shame" (2:25). In today's society sex and shame go together. Often people try to minimize their feelings of shame by convincing themselves that sex outside of God's boundaries is harmless. That animal behavior is acceptable. That rejecting or trashing the image of God is without negative consequences. Wrong!

We shouldn't try to erase the shame for animal behavior. This kind of behavior is shameful for people made in God's image. What we need to do is correct sexual behavior so it is shameless. God wants you to stand naked and unashamed before Him and your "one-flesh" partner.

Treating sex like a plaything is like pretending there are no bullets in a gun when you know it's loaded.

Those who experience sex outside of God's boundaries are mocking God's precious image. They are taking the wonderful gift that separates us from the animal kingdom and dragging it though the mud. People who do this need to feel shame because their behavior is shameful. What they are doing surely grieves the heart of Creator God.

Sex is too powerful to treat lightly. No one has the authority to alter God's design. You cannot use sex as a harmless plaything without serious negative consequences. Ask the teens in the *Prime Time Live* segment who gave it a try and experienced only heartache and pain. Treating sex like a plaything is like pretending there are no bullets in a gun when you know it's loaded. How foolish is that? No matter how hard you pretend, when the gun is fired, the bullets will do their damage.

God made you in His image to raise you above the animals as His special creation. Why would you want to trash the image and act like an animal?

To be "naked and unashamed" does not mean to stuff the shame and guilt. It is not a matter of learning how to manage shame. It is certainly not becoming so hardened that you don't feel appropriate guilt anymore.

The solution is to express your sexuality according to God's plan. To restrict sexual behavior to a lifelong "one-flesh" relationship. Sex within God's established boundaries is a beautiful thing that pleases Him and brings lasting satisfaction.

Chapter 6
Empty Promises, Empty Lives

Heidi had looked forward to this evening for weeks. Chuck, the new guy in school, was coming over to do a little homework and then watch a video. Heidi thought Chuck was great. He was funny and nice and a good athlete. Cute, too!

She had threatened her two younger brothers to leave them alone and not be their usual weird selves. They gave her their word, but the look in their eyes made Heidi's blood boil. She just knew they were brewing up trouble. "You mess this up for me, and I'll make you pay," Heidi warned through clenched teeth. The boys, of course, were paralyzed with fear.

Chuck arrived on time. For a while, all seemed to be going well except for a few minor interruptions from the peanut gallery. Heidi wanted to yell at her brothers, but she was afraid she would turn Chuck off, and managed to say calmly, "Those boys are soooo weird."

Things went downhill from there. When Heidi and Chuck headed for the kitchen to get something to drink and make some popcorn, they found Tyler and Tommy down on all fours, eating cereal out of the dog's dish. They looked up long enough to acknowledge Heidi and Chuck and went right back to lapping up their cereal. Yikes!

Heidi was mortified. "This isn't happening," she mumbled under her breath. "Do they always act like this?" Chuck asked somewhat taken back by this latest antic. "Only when they're awake," she replied with disgust.

No sooner had Heidi and Chuck sat down to watch the video than her brothers, the doggie boys, crawled into the room, barking and sniffing. One had an old shoe in his mouth. The two boys crept across the room, curled up in front of the TV, and chewed on the shoe. Occasionally, they growled and snapped at each other. If looks could kill, Heidi would have terminated Tyler and Tommy on the spot.

Finally, it was too much. Heidi exploded in a fit of rage that sent the doggie boys scurrying for their lives and the popcorn flying everywhere, including all over Chuck.

Well, that did it. "Uh, Heidi," he began cautiously, fearing another eruption. "I've really had a nice time but it's getting late so I'd better be going."

"It's only nine-thirty. Are you sure you have to go so soon?" Heidi replied.

"Yeah, I've got to get up early tomorrow and wash the lawn . . . I mean mow the car . . . I mean . . ."

"I know what you mean. Sorry about the boys. Maybe next time . . . on neutral ground?" she asked hopefully.

"Yeah, maybe," Chuck replied, in a tone that said, *Not in this lifetime!*

Sex for Dummies

Two boys acting like dogs is a bit peculiar. We can't blame Chuck for wondering. While Heidi's little brothers were just being pests, their behavior was still somewhat outside the box. Animal behavior isn't exactly normal for humans, is it?

But what about those who choose to act like animals sexually? They seem to be under the impression that they are with it, liberated, up to date, when in reality they are settling for scraps off the floor. Imagine how God must feel as He watches those made in His image rejecting His gift and feeding like animals. If He responded the way Heidi responded, some folks would be in hot water.

People who promote sexual freedom outside God's boundaries want you to believe they have been set free.

It would be humorous if it weren't so sad to see the actors on television and in movies trying to make animal behavior seem appealing. It's like putting a Rolex watch and diamond jewelry on Jacob, hoping to give my dog some culture and class. Maybe I should think about getting him his own American Express card. Maybe a little after-shave lotion; come to think of it, he'd need a lot of after-shave lotion. No matter how hard I tried, Jacob would never be anything but a dog.

People who promote sexual activity outside God's boundaries want you to believe they have been set free. They have cast off the chains and are experiencing sexual pleasure to the fullest. The truth is, their cup is empty.

A new book, entitled *Sex for Dummies*, is a tip-off to what our culture believes about sex. For those who want to reject the image of God and act like dumb animals, let them go ahead and take the advice of the "experts." But for you, there is a better way. A way that is both God-honoring and personally satisfying.

It's up to you. You must decide if you are going to trash the image of God, or treasure it.

Treasure or Trash?

Years ago one of my daughters spent most of one evening coloring a picture for her teacher at school. She went to bed that night excited at the prospect of giving her teacher this very special gift. But when she came home from school the next day, she was crying. She had given the picture to her teacher as a demonstration of her love, only to find it in the trash can later in the school day, discarded like a worthless piece of scratch paper. My daughter could not understand why someone she cared about so much would throw away a gift that she thought was so special. (We found out later that it was an accident.)

God's gift of sexuality makes us unique among His creatures. It is a treasure. Unlike the teacher who carelessly allowed my daughter's labor of love to drift off her desk and into the trash can, you are expected to prize the treasure God has given.

You have a choice, of course. You are free to disregard the value of your sexuality, or even to use it for trivial pursuits. You can flaunt it, fake it, fantasize about it, or literally forget all about its true worth. If this is your choice, though, you will never experience all that sex was meant to be.

Never Satisfied

Once folks make the choice to ignore the image of God and act like the animals, there begins a lifelong search for significance. Separated from God, they are forced to seek meaning and fulfillment on their own. Groping in the darkness, they run down one blind alley after another. Money. Power. Popularity. Brains. Beauty. Success. Stuff. Some try to dull their pain through drugs and alcohol. Far too many, like Angie, try to find significance through sexual experiences. All this, my friends, is a journey without an end. You see, apart from God, we are *not* significant.

Sex is not making love; it is expressing love.

Society is filled with people trying to find meaning in the arms of passionate lovers. They long for sex to fill the void. But when the party's over and the sun comes up the next morning, they find that whatever satisfaction they may have experienced was temporary at best.

The quest continues for that special lover who will one day bring ecstatic fulfillment. From time to time, for a few brief moments, there is hope before the emptiness returns like a recurring nightmare.

The problem is that sex was never designed by God to meet our need for significance and meaning. Remember? It's like trying to use a car headlight in your living room lamp; it just won't work. Sex, when used to generate significance and meaning in life, will only lead to more despair.

Sex is not the way to make love happen or to find significance. Sex was designed by God to express love and significance. Sex, rather than being the journey to love, is an intimate expression of love. You can't express something you don't already have. Let's put it this way: Love is not *discovered* in the bedroom; it is *demonstrated* in the bedroom. Sex is not "making love"; it is expressing love. When sex becomes a pursuit of something, rather than an expression of something, it will lead to disappointment and despair.

Wrong, Karl!

Karl Marx promoted what he called the "water theory" of sex. He believed our sexual urges are like hunger and thirst. If we are hungry, we eat. If we are thirsty, we drink. If our bodies crave sex, we simply gratify the urge and are satisfied. Marx believed that free and open sex was the answer to sexual need.

Wrong! What he found was just the opposite. The more sexual activity people engaged in, the more they wanted. He created a monster that could never be satisfied.

What drives sexual addiction is the very fact that sex, outside of God's design, does not satisfy.

Because sex, outside of God's design and purpose, cannot satisfy, it becomes more like an addiction. The first time the sexual experience may be pleasant, with a certain amount of excitement and anticipation surrounding it. The next time, it may require more to reach the same "high." After that, I can almost guarantee that it will take more and more to receive less and less.

But the quest is on. Maybe next time it will be better. Maybe next time it will last. At this point, any thought of sex becoming a meaningful expression of love and fulfillment is replaced by a drive for satisfaction. Sex at this level will produce only disappointment. More ominous still is the slippery slope syndrome. This kind of mind-set leads to deviant sexual behavior.

As sex becomes more and more unsatisfactory, people look for new ways to address their pain. This leads to bizarre behavior, including homosexuality, prostitution, rape, and other deviancy. What Karl Marx did not realize was that he was releasing a man-eating lion instead of a lap cat. Sexual freedom has "released" people to suffer a lifetime of emptiness and bondage.

Empty Promises

If we were to personify sex, we would say that sex in our promiscuous culture makes promises it cannot fulfill. Sex is all talk, but no delivery. What do I mean by that? So glad you asked.

Sex lures its victims with promises of love, fulfillment, and ultimately satisfaction. Sex passes itself off as the route to meaning and purpose in life. Sex claims to make the world go 'round. But what sex claims to deliver is a lie! Like the schoolyard bully, when challenged, sex slinks away, powerless to deliver the goods. Sex is filled with empty lies leading to empty lives.

Like alcohol or drugs, sex promises relief from pain. (It is no accident that alcohol and drugs are often linked with sexual misbehavior.) When it's all over and done, the darkness is darker and the pain more intense than before. The whole meaningless dance starts over again, this time with even greater urgency.

A movie portrays some shipwrecked men drifting aimlessly on the ocean in a lifeboat. As the days pass under the scorching sun, their rations of food and fresh water give out. Delirious with thirst, one man ignores all previous warnings, gulps down some salt water while the others are asleep, and dies.

Ocean water contains seven times more salt than the human body can safely ingest. After drinking it, a person becomes dehydrated because the kidneys demand extra water to flush the overload of salt. The more salt water someone drinks, the thirstier he gets. He actually dies of thirst.

Lust is much the same. Desperate for something that appears to be the answer to our need, we don't realize that it is precisely the opposite. In fact, it can kill. So it is with those who believe that sex can fill them with meaning and purpose. In the end, they are empty, shattered by broken promises.

Significance, meaning, and purpose must come from God. He is the ultimate Source. Not sex. Sexuality is an expression of these things, not a pursuit of them. Apart from God and a relationship with Him, sex will never find its rightful place in our lives. Sex simply cannot do what it was never designed to do.

The Need for Change

Have you ever wondered why—if our culture understands sex so well—there is such confusion? Why so much sexual abuse? Why does pornography ensnare so many people? Why does sex sell products? Why is our culture so obsessed with sex? All these things do not point to people who are satisfied but rather to people who are unfulfilled. We are a society driven to experience more—enough is never enough. We are a people chained to a sexual freight train, screaming out of control. It's time we learned how to put on the brakes.

Sex can never take the place of God in our lives.

In a *Time Magazine* article, Manhattan sex therapist Shirley Zussman says, "My patients these days complain about the emptiness of sex without a commitment. Fears of both loneliness and intimacy are a backlash against the 'cool sex' promoted during the sexual revolution." In the same article, psychiatrist Domeena Renshaw, director of the Sexual Dysfunction Clinic at Chicago's Loyola University, states, "Many have tried group sex and the swinging scene, but for them it has been destructive and corrosive."

Well, it's about time. Some "experts" are waking up and smelling the coffee. Some of them are actually confirming what God has been saying all along. That sex outside of God's purpose is unfulfilling and destructive. That sex can never take His place in our lives. That sex apart from God cannot satisfy. That sex must be an expression of fulfillment that is found in God and a celebration of His image. When we lose sight of the image, sex *becomes* God.

Chapter 7
Could You Be Guilty
of Sexual Idolatry?

Imagine yourself on the trip of a lifetime—deep in the jungles of Africa on safari. Your hunting party has made camp, awaiting another day of tracking the king of beasts. About the time you are drifting into dreamland, you are awakened by the sound of drums in the distance. You and your brave companions make your way down a path in the direction of the drums' steady throbbing.

Suddenly you break through the thick underbrush into a clearing, your gaze fixed on an incredible sight. Like a scene straight out of a *National Geographic* special, the natives are dancing around some sort of wooden idol. Both curious and more than a little apprehensive, you drop into a crouched position, squinting your eyes to see more clearly.

Then, as abruptly as it all began, the ceremony comes to an end. The natives look at each other, and someone yells, "Party time!" They break out the refreshments, take their wooden idol, and throw him on the fire like so much cordwood. Next thing you know, they are roasting hot dogs and marshmallows over the blaze. What's going on here? What kind of people would worship such a powerless god?

False Gods

What comes to mind when you think of idol worship? Probably a scenario much like this one—some tribe in a remote corner of the world, paying homage to a handmade image of stone or wood.

The prophet Isaiah painted this word picture:

"The carpenter measures with a line and makes an outline with a marker; he roughs it out with chisels and marks it with compasses. He shapes it in the form of man, of man in all his glory, that it may dwell in a shrine. He cut down cedars, or perhaps took a cypress or oak. He let it grow among the trees of the forest, or planted a pine, and the rain made it grow. It is man's fuel for burning; some of it he takes and warms himself, he kindles a fire and bakes bread. But he also fashions a god and worships it; he makes an idol and bows down to it. Half of the wood he burns in the fire; over it he prepares his meal, he roasts his meat and eats his fill. He also warms himself and says, 'Ah! I am warm; I see the fire.' From the rest he makes a god, his idol; he bows down to it and worships. He prays to it and says, 'Save me; you are my god'" (Isa. 44:13–17).

No way would you be that foolish, right? After all, what civilized person would go out to the woodpile and carve himself a god? Yet the sad truth is, we do it all the time. You see, idolatry is far more than worshiping gods made from wood and stone. Unfortunately, idolatry is alive and well from Wall Street to Walnut Grove.

When you seek meaning and fulfillment in sex rather than in God, you have elevated sex to the place of God in your life.

Time for review. Every person is made in the image of God and created to have a relationship with Him. We find our love, significance, and fulfillment in God. Having met these needs in Him, we can express them in a "one-flesh" sexual relationship within the boundaries of marriage. This is God's plan—the only one that will lead to pleasure and satisfaction. When we follow His plan, sexuality becomes a wonderful celebration of the image of God in us—all it's meant to be.

However, when we choose to trash the image and act more like the animals, sexuality becomes empty, unfulfilling, and destructive. When God is not in His rightful place, there is emptiness inside. Attempts to fill the emptiness with something or someone other than God are a futile effort to create your own god. This is the sin of idolatry.

Millions of people are enslaved to the god of sexuality, a cruel god who refuses to be appeased. When you seek meaning and fulfillment in sex rather than in God, you have elevated sex to the place of God in your life. Sex can be a cruel and deceitful taskmaster. All of which takes us back to the beginning.

Sunrise, Sunset

The apostle Paul reminds us that God's hand is evident in creation: "For since the creation of the world God's invisible qualities—his eternal power and divine nature—have been clearly seen, being understood from what has been made, so that men are without excuse" (Rom. 1:20). God can be seen in the splendor of a sunrise or the awesome fury of a summer storm. He can be seen in the beauty of a peacock or the majesty of a mountain. Remember, God as Creator is an important basis for understanding sexuality.

The fact that the laws of the universe are so predictable that we can send a person to the moon and back with precision timing should assure us that there is a Creator God. To imagine the universe happened by random chance takes far more faith than I can muster!

The real question has to do with what you choose to do with this knowledge. "For although they knew God, they neither glorified him as God nor gave thanks to him, but their thinking became futile and their foolish hearts were darkened. Although they claimed to be wise, they became fools and exchanged the glory of the immortal God for images made to look like mortal man and birds and animals and reptiles" (Rom. 1:21–23).

To see the reality of God and then to deny it is the ultimate act of arrogance by the creature. It's like the clay telling the potter that she doesn't exist even though she has been shaping the clay for hours. It's the computer telling the computer programmer he doesn't count. It's the apple telling the apple tree that the tree doesn't matter. Absurd, of course, but it happens.

Thinking they're really smart and sophisticated, some choose to deny the obvious. When people deny the reality of God's fingerprints all around them, they create their own gods to worship (v. 23). For some, these are actual images of wood or stone. For others, they are the intangible gods of wealth, fame, popularity, and power. For many, this self-made god is the god of sexuality.

Sexual Idolatry

It is no coincidence that Paul goes on to talk about sexual sins (vv. 24–27). When we abandon our belief in God and His image in us, sexual perversions follow. Listen to how Paul's words relate to our discussion of Genesis 1 and 2: "Therefore God gave them over in the sinful desires of their hearts to sexual impurity for the degrading of their bodies with one another. They exchanged the truth of God for a lie, and worshiped and served created things rather than the Creator—who is forever praised" (vv. 24–25).

The "degrading of their bodies" is choosing to act like animals rather than people reflecting the image of God. These people are putting sex on the throne of their lives rather than God. They are creating their own god, then bowing to this self-made deity. They are guilty of worshiping the creature rather than the Creator.

Have It Your Way

How does God respond to such behavior? A stern warning? A slap on the wrist? A lightning bolt from heaven? None of the above. He lets us have our own way—then lets us experience the consequences of our choices.

Like a child who is determined to touch a hot stove, you may have to learn the hard way. In a sense the sexual confusion, pain, abuse, and perversions we see in our society today are a judgment from God. We, as a people, have gotten what we thought we wanted, and the results have been devastating.

Even desire becomes twisted. "Because of this, God gave them over to shameful lusts. Even their women exchanged natural relations for unnatural ones. In the same way the men also abandoned natural relations with women and were inflamed with lust for one another. Men committed indecent acts with other men, and received in themselves the due penalty for their perversion" (vv. 26–27). The word *unnatural* in the original Greek language literally means "against nature." Against nature means against natural design. The sexual perversions in our society oppose God's original design.

This kind of opposition certainly includes homosexual behavior. It is obvious from our anatomy class that men and women were made to fit together. It's also obvious that men don't fit with men and women don't fit with women sexually. If God is Creator—and there is abundant evidence that He is—then the idea of men having sex with men and women with women was never part of His plan.

Take, for example, the common household electrical cord. One end is called a "male" and the other is called a "female." When holding the plug, it's obvious which end goes in the wall socket. You could spend all day trying to plug together two male ends (the end with the prongs), but they would never fit. Not according to manufacturer's design. Even a small child can tell which end of the plug goes into the outlet. The male plug is made to fit the female plug.

Sexual sin is a sin of idolatry.

The argument of Paul in Romans 1 is that when people fail to honor God as God, they reject the image of God and make their own gods. Having made their own gods, sexual perversions follow, even to the extent of going against natural creation design. Once the image is rejected, the door is open for chaos.

Now hear the rest of the story:

"Furthermore, since they did not think it worthwhile to retain the knowledge of God, he gave them over to a depraved mind, to do what ought not to be done. They have become filled with every kind of wickedness, evil, greed and depravity. They are full of envy, murder, strife, deceit and malice. They are gossips, slanderers, God-haters, insolent, arrogant and boastful; they invent ways of doing evil; they disobey their parents; they are senseless, faithless, heartless, ruthless. Although they know God's righteous decree that those who do such things deserve death, they not only continue to do these very things but also approve of those who practice them" (vv. 28–32).

These verses, written in the first century, read like the morning paper! Paul might have been describing our current sex-crazed culture. And he is. God, in His mercy, has sounded this warning down through the centuries to alert His people to the danger of rejecting Him. It's deadly serious stuff. Are you listening?

Sex Education 101

When the Bible lists sins, sexual sin is often at the top of the list. For example, the first three sins listed in Galatians 5:19 as the "acts of the sinful nature" are "sexual immorality, impurity and debauchery (sensuality)." It is also worth noting that the very next sin in line is "idolatry," followed by "witchcraft" (v. 20). Pretty grim company.

Check out Colossians 3:5 while you're at it: "Put to death, therefore, whatever belongs to your earthly nature: sexual immorality, impurity, lust, evil desires and greed which is idolatry." The Bible consistently reminds the reader of the strong tie between the sin of idolatry and sexual perversions. Enough said?

The key to unlocking sex education is not more information about the physical aspect of sex, but rather information about the design and purpose of sex. For sexual behavior to be restored to its proper place of honor, we must first acknowledge God and understand our role as image-bearers. It's not too smart to ignore the spiritual essence of our sexuality.

Smart people ("the wise") understand sex as an expression of fulfillment in God and not a pursuit of fulfillment apart from Him. As the younger brother stated in the "Parable of the Father's Photo": "When you discarded the photo, my poor brother, you forgot the image. When you forgot the image, you forgot what really matters, what satisfies. So you spent your life trying to find what you had thrown away."

In the Bible, we have snapshots of our Heavenly Father, taken by writers inspired by the Holy Spirit to record all we need to know about Him. If we will throw away all our "idols" and focus on His image alone, we will find what really matters, what satisfies.

Chapter 8
Why Sex Was Never Meant to Be a Hit-and-Run

The more we understand the value of our sexuality, the more likely we are to guard it. Sex outside of God's purpose and design devalues us as people made in His image. Such behavior, which is common today, is a way of saying, "I'm not worth much, and neither is my sexuality."

Looking at myself and my sexuality through God's eyes changes everything. If I value my sexuality the way God values it, I will not settle for animal behavior. I will see His design and purpose for sex. I will develop a theology of sexuality to experience all God wants me to experience sexually.

"Wow! That's pretty heavy stuff," you may think. "I've always thought some of those standards about sex were a little rigid, but I figured I'd better get a grip on my hormones so I don't get AIDS or something. I had no idea that what I do with my body makes that much difference to God."

Once we understand the value of sex and the honor of being made in God's image, our perspective changes. Suddenly He isn't a cosmic killjoy, waiting to ruin all our fun with His rules. He is the Creator God who actually makes it possible to express love in a "one-flesh" relationship filled with passion and meaning. The theology of sex is necessary to recapture the wonder of sex. It is the route to restoring the value of our sexuality as God intended. It's the secret to lasting pleasure.

Believe it or not, sexuality pictures some of the most significant truths about God in all the Bible.

Three in One

Take the Trinity, for example. What does understanding God as a Trinity have to do with your sex life? Plenty. Remember our discussion of Genesis 1:1? In that verse we were introduced to God as a plural Being. The name used for God in the first verse of the Bible is *Elohim*, which is a plural name. It does not mean "three," but it does mean "more than one." This name is used more than 2,300 times in the Old Testament alone.

The concept of plurality is balanced with the idea that God is also one God. "Hear, O Israel: The LORD our God, the LORD is one" (Deut. 6:4). What made the Hebrew people unique in ancient times was that they were monotheistic (believed in one God) rather than polytheistic (believed in many gods) like the heathen nations around them.

Now stay with me. While the Bible clearly teaches that God is one God, this one God is also a plurality. Both Matthew and Luke, in the New Testament, identify God as Father, Son, and Holy Spirit—*three Persons, yet one God* (Matt. 28:19; Luke 3:21–22). Time out for brain cramp!

Just so you won't feel alone in your frustration, let me hasten to say that no one can really ever fully understand how three can be one. But it's important to try. We have already discussed that the ability of God to be relational—existing in community with Himself—is part of His image in us. As He relates to Himself and to us, so we can relate to others. But how does it work?

Some try to illustrate the Trinity by using the analogy of an egg. An egg has a white, a yolk, and a shell—three parts, yet one egg. The problem is that the yolk is not the egg, the shell is not the egg, and the white is not the egg. Only together do the three parts make up an egg.

Nice try, but it's not quite the same thing. While we cannot grasp the wonder of God as a Trinity, we can move one step closer to understanding through His design for sexuality. The "one-flesh" relationship is the best illustration of the Trinity.

One Plus One Equals One

By now you know this one by heart: "For this reason a man will leave his father and mother and be united to his wife, and they will become one flesh" (Gen. 2:24). Two people—a man and his wife—become one. There you have it! Two shall become one. Not two halves becoming one whole, but two complete individuals becoming one—together.

This "becoming one flesh" is the sexual union. In some supernatural act, understood fully only by God, two separate people become one. Somehow, this plurality, defined as "male and female," is also a picture of the Trinity—God in three Persons.

The Glue

"For this reason a man will leave his father and mother and be united to his wife, and they will become one flesh." To be "united" means to be "glued together." Be patient with me. I know we've covered this before, but it's so important I must repeat it once again. Sexuality is like a glue that bonds two people together. Sex unites a couple in a way that is unique to any other relationship. Not to say that sex alone can hold a marriage together. It's not that easy. But sex does provide a powerful Super-Glue. It's this gluing of two people that provides some experiential understanding of how God can be three in one.

If you take two pieces of plywood and glue them together with wood glue, they are united. Once the glue has dried, just try pulling those two pieces of wood apart. No way—it's as if they were always one. They will never again be separate pieces as they were before. Oh, you could probably separate them with a crowbar, but it won't be a clean break. The pieces will tear and expose the jagged scars—because once glued together, they are meant to stay together.

Recently I pulled a couple of pictures off my office wall. I had used two-sided tape to put them up. At first I'd hung them on a nail, but they were crooked, so I used the tape. After that, they hung straight and true. But when I wanted to remove them, guess what? Yep! Part of the drywall came with them. Ouch!

This is why divorce is so painful. Divorce is a ripping of something God never intended to come apart. The "one flesh"—the uniting or "gluing" as designed by God—is a beautiful thing. If used properly, it creates the most intimate relationship humanly possible. But when used apart from His plan, the gluing is a destructive force.

Remember some of the comments made by the teens on the *Prime Time Live* segment, "Sex, Truth, and Videotape"? One girl confessed, "It was one of the worst experiences of my life!" Another admitted, "It just made me feel so horrible and, like, so dirty." Ask yourself, if sex were merely a pleasurable physical experience, why so much pain?

It is obvious that sexuality goes far beyond the mere physical act. Something is happening in that experience that is very intense and very permanent—the gluing process. When sex takes place outside of God's boundaries, there is a gluing and a tearing He never intended.

The gluing effect is what makes marriage so special. It is something you should be willing to share with no one else except your "one-flesh" partner. The reason people cannot have sex and walk away without pain is that God never meant for it to be that way. He never planned it to be a hit-and-run experience. What is so mighty to teach us about God is also hurtful when misused.

Yadá, Yadá, Yadá

Not only does sex picture God as Trinity, it also pictures the depth of intimacy He wants with us. It helps explain why He wired us with a sex drive in the first place. The intimacy between God and His people, illustrated by sexual union between a husband and wife, is but a small taste of what is possible with God. He has designed us with strong sexual longings to draw us to Himself. It is only when we are intimate with Him that we are truly satisfied.

The Hebrew word for "know," *yadá*, is often used in referring to sexual relations in the Old Testament. "And Adam *knew* Eve his wife; and she conceived, and bare Cain" (Gen. 4:1 KJV). We see this again in 1 Samuel 1:19–20: "Elkanah *knew* Hannah his wife; and the LORD remembered her. Wherefore it came to pass, when the time was come about after Hannah had conceived, that she bare a son" (KJV). Most of the modern translations have replaced the term *know* with "had relations with" (NASB) or "lay with" (NIV) or some other more explicit phrase.

Sexuality is a picture of God's desire to have an intimate personal relationship with us.

While these phrases may clarify the meaning of the verse in its context, it is important that the theological concept of "know" not be lost somewhere in the translation. It's no accident that the term *yadá*, "to know," is used both of human sexual relations and when referring to God's intimacy with His people.

This is also true in the New Testament. For example, in Matthew 1:25 we read, "But he had no union with her until she gave birth to a son." This verse refers to Jesus' parents not having sexual relations until after His birth. The Greek text literally reads: "He [Joseph] did not know her." That word *know* again. The word that also means God's deep relationship with believers.

There is a constant reminder in both the Old and New Testaments that sexuality is a picture of God's desire for an intimate personal relationship with us. This is seen again in the lengthy instructions to husbands and wives in Ephesians 5:22–33:

"Wives, submit to your husbands as to the Lord. For the husband is the head of the wife as Christ is the head of the church, his body, of which he is the Savior. Now as the church submits to Christ, so also wives should submit to their husbands in everything.

"Husbands, love your wives, just as Christ loved the church and gave himself up for her to make her holy, cleansing her by the washing with water through the word, and to present her to himself as a radiant church, without stain or wrinkle or any other blemish, but holy and blameless. In this same way, husbands ought to love their wives as their own bodies. He who loves his wife loves himself. After all, no one ever hated his own body, but he feeds and cares for it, just as Christ does the church—for we are members of his body. 'For this reason a man will leave his father and mother and be united to his wife, and the two will become one flesh.' This is a profound mystery—but I am talking about Christ and the church. However, each one of you also must love his wife as he loves himself, and the wife must respect her husband."

Do you see the connection? The husband's role as a picture of Christ? The wife's role as a picture of the church? Husband and wife, two lovers, illustrating how Christ loves His people, the Church.

And did you notice the deliberate repetition of Genesis 2:24? After quoting the Old Testament reference to the "one-flesh" relationship," Paul adds: "This is a profound mystery—but I am talking about Christ and the church" (Eph. 5:32). For all you guys who thought your wives were a mystery or you women who had the same idea about your husbands, there is a much more profound mystery here! Paul specifically identifies the sexual union in marriage, then carefully connects this concept with Christ and His Church.

And what about that other rather graphic picture Paul painted for the Corinthians? "Do you not know that he who unites himself with a prostitute is one with her in body? For it is said, 'The two will become one flesh.' But he who unites himself with the Lord is one with him in spirit" (1 Cor. 6:16–17).

Paul uses the same language to describe sexual intimacy that he uses to describe the union between Christ and His people. The tie between the two relationships is unmistakable.

Another evidence of this relationship between our sexuality and God's desire to be intimate with us is His description of spiritual unfaithfulness. He calls it spiritual adultery, picturing Himself as the faithful lover who has been jilted by an adulterous partner. The entire Book of Hosea uses this imagery: an unfaithful wife representing unfaithful Israel, and a faithful, loving, forgiving husband representing our faithful, loving, and forgiving God.

It's easy, then, to see why God responds so strongly to sexual immorality. Any sexual activity outside of His "one-flesh" partnership design misrepresents His relationship with His people. When you indulge in sexual immorality, you are misrepresenting God. God is not a fickle Lover. God is not a selfish Lover, using people for His own pleasure. God is not a hit-and-run Lover. He is a faithful Lover who will always be devoted to His people.

When we sin sexually, we are distorting the truth related to the character of God.

It is no surprise that God takes this subject seriously, since what is at stake is far more than the abuse of physical pleasure. What is at stake is the reputation of God Himself. When we sin sexually, we are distorting the truth related to His character.

Woe to those who make choices that portray God as an unfaithful Lover!

It's Up to You

God has designed significant pictures of Himself into your sexuality. What is powerful for good is also powerful for evil. You have a choice. One choice results in sexual fulfillment far beyond anything you can imagine. More than that, it provides enough of a taste of intimacy to fill us with a deeper passion to know God. It is the celebration of His image. Far from keeping you strait-jacketed, this choice sets you free from guilt and the baggage from other relationships, and denies Satan a foothold in your life.

The consequences of the other choice—to use sexuality outside God's intended boundaries—are frightening. No way can you subject yourself to the uniting and tearing for an extended period of time, or even *once*, and escape pain and destruction. It's a sure thing.

If you choose to continue to be involved in sexual activity outside God's design, then you will have to insulate yourself from the intense "tearing" pain. To do this, you must close off your heart. Thus, sex becomes merely a physical act. Your heart is buried deep within a protective shell. This is what makes sex the meaningless dance it is for so many.

Buried Alive

Human behavior is never more like animal behavior than when a person reaches this level of sexual interaction and is totally detached from the experience. There is no chance of fulfillment or real satisfaction or even giving and receiving love when emotions are shrouded in darkness and shut down.

People who live like this have become cold, calloused, and blinded to the serious consequences of their choices. They try new ways to make sex more exciting and fulfilling, which leads to all kinds of perversions. What is lacking is not a better technique. What is lacking is recognizing that this route is all wrong and will never be right. That only repenting—turning around—and heading in the direction of God's best can bring ultimate satisfaction. That what they are doing now is settling for Satan's lie when they could be living life to the max.

Parable of the Dancing Puppet

Parable of the Dancing Puppet

✝

Once upon a time, in a land far away, there was a sleepy little village. It was a place of quiet contentment, far removed from the noise and clutter of the cities. In the heart of the village, at the end of a winding cobblestone street, there lived a woodcarver. He was known for his ability to turn ordinary pieces of wood into extraordinary creations. In his hands, a stick became a pony. A log became a footstool. A branch became the leg of a chair. People traveled for miles to purchase these works of art.

But of all the items he crafted, he most enjoyed making toys. Though he had never married and had no children of his own, the old woodcarver loved to see the village children laugh and play. He made flutes and games and puzzles. He made rocking horses and toy soldiers and dolls so lifelike they appeared as if they might speak.

His favorite was a lovely little marionette—a puppet whose wooden body would come to life when the master toy maker worked the strings. She was dressed as an elegant dancer in ballerina shoes and tights and a beautiful sky-blue dress. In her hair silk bows shimmered in the sunlight. She was beautiful indeed.

The old woodcarver had often imagined that, if he had had a daughter, she might look something like this doll—graceful and sensitive and charming. He had taken special pains with her face, painting on eyes that seemed to twinkle with delight and a smile that warmed the hearts of all who entered his quaint little shop.

Those who visited often remarked upon the little dancer. Many wanted to buy her, but she was not for sale. Not at any price. She was his special creation. On one occasion a wealthy gentleman, looking for the perfect gift for a beloved granddaughter, offered more money than could be made in a year. But the gentle craftsman was not tempted in the least. No, this doll, who had in some way taken the place of the children he would never have, must stay.

One particularly lonely night, as the old man sat at his workbench with the moonlight streaming through an open window, he wished, just once, that the little dancer could know how much he loved her. Silly, of course, to love a toy. But he did all the same. If only she could dance for him one night . . . .

What happened next is hard to say. A breeze began to blow softly through the open window. This was no ordinary wind, to be sure. No, it seemed more like a celestial breath. Both frightened and fascinated, the toy maker sat transfixed. He found himself staring into the eyes of the beautiful dancer as if the puppet could explain this strange and wondrous event.

As he looked, it seemed as if she looked back. At first he laughed it off as the mere musings of an old man's mind. But upon closer inspection, he could see that some kind of transformation had taken place. As he reached out to touch her delicate wooden features, painted so skillfully with his brushes, his heart began to race wildly. She was alive—of that there was no doubt!

Although her face was now filled with expression mere paint brushes could never have produced, her arms and legs lay limp on the table. Carefully, he picked up the wooden dowels that held her strings and began to work them, allowing her hands and feet to move. The more he worked them, the more she seemed destined to dance. They laughed and sang together as she pirouetted across the table, again and again. What was happening, he could not say for sure, but questions could wait. The hours together might be few, and this was a time for celebration. His wish had been granted!

Into the night the toy maker guided each step of the dancer in perfect rhythm with the melody of a music box he also had crafted. After hours of pleasure, he excused himself to fix a cup of cinnamon tea. When he returned, he noticed that the little doll was lying where he had left her. But something was different. The expression on her face had changed as she eyed the other dolls sitting on a shelf nearby, waiting to be claimed by new owners.

"Why should I have these strings when all the others are free?" she asked petulantly. "How shall I ever be able to dance where I wish?"

The toy maker tried to explain that the strings had been attached as a special act of love. No other doll had been crafted with such care. "The strings are not intended to restrict your movements, my dear," he said, "only to enable you to move at all."

But she was adamant and pursed her little mouth in a pout. She became so obsessed with the strings that she no longer wanted to dance with her creator. What had been so pleasurable before was now forgotten in the pursuit of something more.

The old toy maker shook his head sadly. Couldn't she see that the other dolls were not alive? Hadn't she noticed that she could move about easily and joyfully in the hands of the master craftsman? But, alas, she could not,—or would not—see. Finally, with great reluctance, he gave her what she wished. He took out his knife and, with tears in his eyes, prepared to cut her free.

As the cords were severed, one by one, she began to crumble lifelessly to the bench. First one arm dangled to her side, then the other. Then her legs. At first, her face radiated happiness over her newfound freedom. But as she fell, tangled in a useless heap, her expression turned to one of confusion, then to alarm. What had she done?

For the first time, she studied the other dolls on the shelf. There was no life in them. Why hadn't she noticed before? Without strings, she could not move. With fearful eyes, she peered back into the face of her creator. She yearned to twirl and spin, but alas, she had rejected the one who had set her feet to dancing.

The toy maker sobbed himself to sleep in his big chair. In the morning, when he awoke, he was convinced that he had been dreaming. Such things didn't happen. Puppets didn't come to life!

About the time he had persuaded himself, a customer entered the shop. As she stood at the counter, she glanced over at the little dancer, crumpled on the table. "Such a forlorn face for such a lovely doll," she observed. Indeed the countenance had changed. No longer did the eyes sparkle, and there was no smile on the painted lips.

With a lump in his throat, the old woodcarver picked up the puppet to assess the damage. As he did so, the strings fell to the ground.

"Is she broken?" the customer inquired.

"Yes. Until her strings are reattached, she will not dance."

"Oh, but surely she can be repaired!"

"Perhaps," the toy maker mumbled sadly as he put the doll in a box and returned to his work. "Perhaps."

Chapter 9
When Satan Pulls the Strings

A friend of mine once found himself in a sticky situation. He was walking down a street in Chicago late one night when he stumbled onto a tense scene—a gang fight, just about to erupt.

"Whose side are you on?" someone demanded.

"Oh, nobody's," he gulped. "I just wandered in here by mistake."

About that time the other gang showed up, and he was able to duck out. Whew! Too close for comfort!

All of us must decide whose side we're on in the area of sexuality. God's archenemy, Satan, was one of His top angels in heaven, a beautiful creature. But when Satan decided he wanted God's glory for himself, to be worshiped like God, he and his evil angels were cast out of heaven forever.

Satan lives to mock God and all He stands for.

Since that time, Satan's number-one goal has been to pull others down with him and to blind them to the truth about God and about themselves. Enter Adam and Eve. It was Satan in the form of a serpent who appeared in their garden paradise and duped them with the same lie that had cost him his heavenly abode. Satan believed he could ascend to the heavens and be like God. He found out he was wrong. Yet he used the same lie to deceive Adam and Eve. He convinced them that they could be like God and decide for themselves what is right and wrong, that they could rewrite God's rules. Wrong again. The sin of Adam and Eve brought pain and death and plunged the human race into sin. The sin of prideful disobedience is the sin of declaring ourselves to be God.

Satan's Game Plan

From the time of his fall, Satan has been out to mock God and destroy people. He accomplishes both with one clever lie: You can be like God (Gen. 3:5). He hates it when people honor and serve God, and is delighted when they believe the lie and rebel against Him.

In the area of sexuality, many people today believe that they can rewrite the rules. Satan uses people like pawns in a chess match to play his sinister game. He lures his victims in with false promises, then sneers at their misery and pain. He doesn't care about anyone; he is incapable of love and compassion. If, through lies and deception, he can use you to mock God, he'll do it in a heartbeat. In the process, when your life is destroyed, he'll discard you like a piece of useless trash.

Idolatry, we have learned, is Satan's attempt to divert our worship from God to worthless idols, whether tangible or intangible. Technically, any worship that is not given to God goes to Satan; there really is no middle ground.

One of Satan's most effective tools, if not *the* most effective, is sexual sin. How he must sneer and hiss with satisfaction when he can con people, especially those who claim to know the Lord, into mocking God and dragging His image through the mire of sexual sinfulness. He must get a real kick when people believe his lies and put sex on the throne of their lives. But he won't be completely satisfied until he has destroyed you—completely. And it begins with deception.

A Spiritual Battle

Those who claim that sex is nothing more than a physical act between two consenting adults are deceived. Sex is deeply spiritual and reflects a battle between God and Satan, a battle that has gone on for millennia. The issues go far deeper than the use or misuse of your body. They involve the choice of whether you will use every aspect of your life—physical, mental, emotional, moral—to glorify God or to side with Satan as he seeks to deflect God's glory to himself.

What a privilege to be an image-bearer for God. No other creature bears His image like you do. But when you engage in sex outside God's boundaries, you soil the image. You can also soil the image by failing to register disapproval when someone else is playing fast and loose with God's beautiful gift. When others mock God in movies or on television, you participate when you willingly allow those scenes to burn themselves into your brain. When you dwell on magazine or Internet pictures in which sex is reduced to animal behavior, you stamp those images with your approval. When you fill your mind with sexually explicit song lyrics, you join those creative people who offend God with their music.

Sexual sin should offend us because it mocks the God who loves us and set us apart from the rest of creation. Rather than being seduced and enticed by the sexual perversions of the world, we should be sickened by what others are doing to God's special gift.

Resisting sexual sin is not just a matter of will power or self-discipline or just saying no, as important as these things are. The key to sexual purity is to see sexuality through God's eyes. To be offended by what offends God. To be hurt by what hurts God. To be motivated to honor God with your sex life because you have a dynamic love relationship with Him.

This internal, relationship-based motivation to resist sexual temptation is the most effective way to experience victory. We want to do more than just manage our sin; we want to be offended by sin. We must do more than simply resist sinful desires; we must replace those sinful desires with a stronger desire to find pleasure in God rather than pleasure apart from Him.

One way to go on the offense against sexual sin is to be alert to Satan's tactics. He is the "father of lies," so truth is the antidote. We need to attack every form of lying, including misrepresentation of the truth.

Liar! Liar!

I know of one Heisman Trophy winner whose story was told at the halftime of a college bowl game. The reporter mentioned that this football star had grown up in the ghetto fighting for his life. Because of poverty and violence, supposedly at the hands of his dysfunctional family, he had barely survived.

A few days later, when interviewed on a local TV station, the player was asked about the report. The young man shrugged. "I was wondering whose story they were telling. It sure wasn't mine." Come to find out, he

85

had grown up in a middle-class home with loving parents in a nice neighborhood. The reporter had falsified the facts in order to tell a more dramatic story, and the football player was unhappy that his family had been embarrassed on national TV.

Being misrepresented is a terrible thing, especially when there is no way to set the record straight. Recently Tom Osborne, the former football coach at the University of Nebraska, published a book entitled *On Solid Ground*. When asked why he had written it, he said, "It's like looking at a picture hanging crooked on the wall. After a while you want to straighten it out."

Tom was referring to the way he has been misquoted by the press since winning his national championships. I happen to know about Coach Osborne. He is a man of integrity and honor and doesn't deserve this kind of misrepresentation.

Currently I am embroiled in another controversy related to a friend of mine, another coach at the University of Nebraska. He, too, is being unfairly portrayed in the local and national media. I even appeared on ESPN's *Sportscenter* to endorse my friend's character.

How sad that you can spend your life as a model of respectability, only to have the media make up dirt just to sell a story, or worse, to push an agenda. Thankfully, God is our Judge, not the secular press.

Sexual sin presents a picture of God that simply isn't true.

But what does all this have to do with sexuality? Good question. We Nebraskans are known for our passion for football. But we can be equally passionate about justice and fairness. If there is anyone who should not be misrepresented, it's God. Sexual sin presents a picture of God that simply isn't true.

False Advertising

How must God feel when His character is so consistently distorted? Sexual sin takes that sublime and beautiful image of deity and soils and dirties it until it is barely recognizable.

How could this happen? Because so many people, unaware of their real longing—for intimacy with God—try to fulfill that longing with sexual intimacy. They put on their party hats and their eat-drink-and-be-merry mind-sets and act like they're having a ball. Their own sexual appetites fuel their search for satisfaction. Not finding it, they keep looking in all the wrong places. Sexual addiction becomes sexual idolatry. And idolatry, as you already know, is a journey to destruction.

Meanwhile, the picture of God as Trinity is marred by the graffiti of sexual sin. What might have helped us understand how God can be Three in One—the "one-flesh" relationship of a husband and wife—is now spoiled. Looking on, the world is more confused than ever. Rather than using sexuality to help us know God better, it is used to drive ourselves—and others—farther from Him.

God wants to be as intimate with us as a husband is with his wife, as tender and loving. God doesn't just want us to know *about* Him; He wants us to know Him personally and intimately. How tragic when God's image is carelessly portrayed to the world, especially when it is people in His own family who so often participate in the distortion.

How would you feel if someone in your family consistently misrepresented you? Would you sue? Punch him out? Write her out of the will?

If God spoke the world into being, He could just as easily wipe out the human race with a whisper. He certainly has a legal case against those who choose to advertise Him falsely. I'm not a lawyer, but I know enough to know that the case would hold up in court. As for the Father's will? There are rewards for those who obey Him and judgment for those unbelievers who don't. But even believers can lose their rewards, and there is always the burden of a guilty conscience.

We can be thankful that God is a merciful God and that "His mercy endures forever." He is not vengeful. He won't retaliate when we fail Him. But even though repentant sinners are forgiven for their sins, they are left with scars that will never quite go away.

Straight Talk about Sex

Let's be honest with one another. As a culture we are in the midst of a sexual crisis. There are those who say that what people do behind closed doors is their own business, and no one gets hurt. That couldn't be further from the truth. I deal with the sexual carnage every week. It would be easier to talk about who *isn't* getting hurt.

I sit and listen to the woman whose heart is broken because her husband is addicted to pornography. What he does in the privacy of their own home is destroying their marriage and alienating him from her and the children. And for what? For a few fleeting moments of pleasure that does nothing but leave him dissatisfied and desperate for more. More of what? More pictures and images of someone who doesn't even know his name, doesn't care that he has a heartbeat. Someone who would be totally indifferent if he were diagnosed with terminal cancer today. Is this a good reason to throw away a wife and family—a whole lifetime? Is this really experiencing more?

And what about the dad who sits with his face buried in his hands because he is too ashamed to look me in the eye. He's ashamed because I've just informed him that I know he's been sexually molesting his daughter. He can't even believe it himself—that he could treat his little girl like a pimp would treat his prostitute! She's not Daddy's little angel anymore. May never be again. Tell *that* dad that no one gets hurt in this free-wheeling, sexually crazed culture of ours.

Then there's the girl who dreamed of college, husband, and family, but at sixteen, found herself pregnant and alone. The abortion didn't go well and now she has no chance of having any more children. Her guilt over the abortion and her hatred of men is causing her to withdraw into depression and thoughts of suicide. It was only a one-night stand, and she thought no one would ever know.

I sit with the husband who now must raise his small children alone because his wife decided she needed a better lover. She bought the lie and today is gone to who knows where, doing who knows what, and the children ask, "Daddy, how come Mommy doesn't love us anymore?"

We've come too far together in this study to pretend these testimonies aren't true. I meet these people every week. I hear their sad stories every time I share the theology of sexuality with a group. I talk with them. I cry with them, and I attempt to help them pick up the pieces by the grace of God. Even now, I can hear the echo of the many voices of those who, with lifeless eyes, have said, "Why didn't someone tell me these things before?"

Let's face it. The Deceiver has been far more effective with his message than those who speak for God. The Church often finds herself more into crisis management than crisis prevention. The body count is rising. People are dying. Something must change before we self-destruct. It's time to clear the confusion before one more person believes the lie and has to suffer the consequences.

Now What?

What if you have already experienced sex outside of God's boundaries? Is it too late for you? Are you like the wooden ballerina who came alive in the master carver's hands, only to find that she was not content with his company alone? Have you danced with the devil?

---

*It is possible to put the strings of your life
back in the Master's hands.*

If so, it is possible to put the strings of your life back in the Master's hands. Seeing sex through God's eyes is a critical move in the right direction—but it's only the first step in the dance. There is practical help for learning how to follow His lead until the ball is over.

Chapter 10
Pleasure with a Price Tag

In the swinging '70s, a book entitled *Open Marriage* attempted to legitimize deviant sexual behavior in marriage by suggesting that spouses simply be open and honest about it. Interestingly, it was a reporter for *The Washington Post*, Richard Cohen, who challenged this dangerous theory, as quoted in Chuck Swindoll's excellent book, *Strike the Original Match:*

> "*Open Marriage*, by George and Nena O'Neil, was a book for the times and it said over and over again that you should be honest, straight, out-front, give space, let the other person do their thing, communicate and if you wanted to have an affair . . . do be honest about it—don't sneak around, make excuses, call late in the afternoon with some cock-and-bull story about work. Simply pick up the phone and say, 'Honey, I'll be a bit late tonight. I'm going to have an affair.'

> "But there were these couples I know. They were open, they were honest. They were having affairs. They were not sneaking around (applause), they were not lying (applause), they were being honest (whistles). They were being open. Everyone agreed that it was wonderful. The men agreed and the women agreed and I agreed and it all made you wonder. Then they split. There was something wrong. Invariably, someone couldn't take it. It has nothing to do with the head. The head understood. It was the heart; it was, you should pardon the expression, broken.

"It all made you think. It made you think that maybe there are things we still don't know about men and women and maybe before we spit in the eye of tradition, we ought to know what we are doing. I have some theories and one of them is that one of the ways you measure love is not with words but with actions—with commitment, with what you are willing to give up, with what you are willing to share with no one else."

Richard Cohen was on the right track. But the O'Neils were doing more than merely spitting on tradition; they were spitting on God's original design and purpose for sexuality. They were seeking to redefine its boundaries and justify animal behavior.

Proceed with Caution!

Sexuality does not come without warning labels. When you buy a product that has a warning label on it, do you consider that label to be protective or restrictive? In other words, do you look at a label that says, "WARNING! POISON! FATAL IF SWALLOWED!" and think, *How dare they tell me what to do? Who do they think they are anyway?* No. Most rational people appreciate the warning lest they make a fatal error.

Look at it this way: Without warning labels, you would not have more freedom, but less. The label identifies that which should be avoided and sets us free to enjoy that which is good. Knowing the truth ahead of time is better than not knowing.

God is the Author of pleasure, the Creator of our sexuality. Sexuality is a good gift that teaches us rich theology about God. But sexuality also comes with a warning label: "DANGER! USE ONLY AS DIRECTED BY GOD. If MISUSED, THIS GIFT WILL LEAD TO EXTREME PAIN!"

Having read the warning label, you are now free to experience the joy and freedom of sex within God's boundaries. Rather than having to guess where the land mines are, you now know so that you can move forward with confidence.

Here Comes the Judge

For those who refuse to pay attention to the warning label, there is trouble brewing. Some of the most devastating judgments in the Bible seem to relate to some form of sexual sin. The evil that was rampant when God judged the earth with a universal flood was sexual in nature (see Gen. 6).

One of the sins, if not *the* sin, that brought on the judgment and destruction of Sodom and Gomorrah was sexual (see Gen. 19). Sexual sin brought about a number of bizarre judgments in the nation of Israel (check out Gen. 29, 34, and 38 and Judges 19 for other examples). And sexual sin continued to be a serious problem with devastating consequences for the New Testament church (1 Cor. 5:1). Failure to read the warning label is costly.

It boggles the mind to consider that sexual sin breaks at least half of the Ten Commandments! As we have discussed, sexual sin makes pleasure a god, which violates the first commandment, "You shall have no other gods before me" (Ex. 20:3). According to Romans 1, sexual sin is a sin of idolatry, which violates the command "You shall not make for yourself an idol . . . . You shall not bow down to them or worship them" (Ex. 20:4–5). Sexual sin often includes adultery, which violates the seventh commandment (v. 14). Sexual sin is taking something that doesn't belong to you, which violates the eighth commandment (v. 15). Sexual sin often involves coveting something—or someone—that doesn't belong to you, which violates the command "You shall not covet your neighbor's wife" (v. 17). Beyond these, sexual sin dishonors your parents, often includes lying, and in some cases even leads to violence and murder (2 Sam. 11).

Sexual sin breaks at least half of the Ten Commandments.

Whatever God has given you for good, Satan will attempt to sabotage or divert for his evil purposes. That is why you must be so careful to read the warning label and not misuse God's wonderful gift. Why suffer the unnecessary pain of trial and error when He has clearly marked the pathway to pleasure?

Truth that Sets You Free

Having discovered the theology of sexuality, your desire should be to experience sexuality in a way that is pleasing to God. It's a win-win proposition.

Paul has told us that God's will for our lives is that we remain sexually pure. In other words, that we experience sex within God's boundaries and according to His design. Read carefully! Lock in these words:

"It is God's will that you should be sanctified: that you should avoid sexual immorality; that each of you should learn to control his own body in a way that is holy and honorable, not in passionate lust like the heathen, who do not know God; and that in this matter no one should wrong his brother or take advantage of him. The Lord will punish men for all such sins, as we have already told you and warned you. For God did not call us to be impure, but to live a holy life. Therefore, he who rejects this instruction does not reject man but God, who gives you his Holy Spirit" (1 Thess. 4:3–8).

Did you get that? Purity is not just one man's opinion. Paul sounded the warning, but it was God's idea, and when we reject "this instruction," we are turning our backs on God Himself!

The road to sexual purity begins with understanding the theology of sexuality. The society in which we live tries to make illicit sex as appealing as possible. You are constantly enticed to believe the lie that you can be satisfied sexually apart from God's blueprint. But in the end, you are only enticed to journey down a pathway of destruction.

The writer of Proverbs says it well:

"My son, pay attention to my wisdom, listen well to my words of insight, that you may maintain discretion and your lips may preserve knowledge. For the lips of an adulteress drip honey, and her speech is smoother than oil; but in the end she is bitter as gall, sharp as a double-edged sword. Her feet go down to death; her steps lead straight to the grave. She gives no thought to the way of life; her paths are crooked, but she knows it not" (Prov. 5:1–6).

Notice the use of male and female pronouns in the seductive scene played out in this proverb. These pronouns do not imply that only women do the seducing and that only men are vulnerable. These words are simply personifying sexual temptation.

The writer uses graphic terms to make his case. The lips of the seductress "drip with honey, and her speech is smoother than oil." She says what she knows you want to hear. She knows what buttons to push. She customizes her allurement to draw you into her web of destruction.

The serpent was the original seductress, "more crafty than any of the wild animals" (Gen. 3:1). To be crafty means to be clever or shrewd. The enemy of our souls is shrewd. He knows how to scratch where you itch.

That's what makes him so effective.

This also explains why temptation and deception are so easy to spot in your life, but why I might be blind to it in mine. To remain sexually pure, we need each other. I can help spot deception in your life while you look for it in mine. Together we are much wiser than we are apart. We can hold one another accountable against the "double-edged sword" of the enemy. The seductress is good; we must be better.

For example, as this proverb points out, beware of the smooth talker who uses euphemisms for sin. "A harmless little flirtation" for "fornication." "Significant other" or "sex partner" instead of "husband" or "wife." "Affair" instead of "adultery." Talk that's "smoother than oil"? Yeah, *snake* oil, straight from the serpent in the Garden of Eden. Lies. All lies.

Sexual Correctness

When you allow yourself to believe the lie, you will continuously struggle with sexual temptation. If you incorrectly think you are missing out on real pleasure by following God's plan, you're on a dangerous precipice. Eventually you will take a fall and suffer the painful consequences.

You must believe that all you are missing out on when following God's design is pain and heartache. If you are determined to obey God's command and honor Him with your body, you will struggle continually if you do not think rightly about sex. Good intentions mixed with wrong beliefs spells disaster. Know the truth. God tells the truth always. Don't believe the lie of the culture. Outside of God's plan, you will experience less, not more. Believe it!

Picture a magazine ad showing a good-looking man or a beautiful woman who promises a glorious night of sexual delight. Imagine that you are tempted to respond. The temptation is great because you are being promised something that isn't true—a fantasyland that doesn't exist. Now imagine that you learn that this model in the magazine ad has lured your dad or mom away and destroyed your family. Now, you would see the whole thing differently. This person destroyed something you cared about very deeply and now you are reaping the heartache. In some ways, your family would never be the same again.

Knowing the truth would make the ad far less appealing. Most likely, you would be disgusted by this sleazy come-on. You don't think people believe these lies? I have sat and listened to countless stories of men and women who have traded a few minutes of pleasure for years of heartache and bondage. Not one time has anyone ever mentioned that the moments of pleasure were worth the price. The pleasure is momentary, but the pain can linger for a lifetime.

Recognizing the promotion of sexuality in our culture for what it is provides the backbone for resisting temptation. When you understand the theology of sexuality, you can never view sexual temptation in the same way again. Rather than seeing through the cloudy haze of enticement to pleasure, the aftermath—pain and suffering—stands out in bold relief. Instead of life on the edge, illicit sex becomes mockery of God. Rather than being an exciting and glamorous adventure, casual sex is seen as an indignity than breaks His heart. Rather than hearing the clever and alluring words of the seductress, you hear the sneering of Satan as he seeks to involve you in demeaning the God you love.

When you are thinking correctly, according to God's definition of reality, you should be outraged by every invitation to exploit your sexuality. You should be livid over the trashing of something so beautiful.

To think that creatures could inform the Creator on sexuality and pleasure is laughable.

Let the Good Times Roll

When the self-proclaimed "sex experts" endeavor to portray God as irrelevant to the discussion of sex, we need to remember who created it. Remember? God's first recorded command to Adam and Eve in the Garden was to have sex. A perfect couple in a perfect environment, celebrating the goodness of God. It doesn't get any better than that. To think that creatures could inform the Creator about sexuality and pleasure is laughable.

In a feature article entitled "Not Frenzied, But Fulfilled," a *Newsweek* writer dispels several commonly held myths surrounding sex. One of those myths is that "sex—or at least the frequent and deeply satisfying kind—belongs mostly to those who are single, unattached and adventuresome between the sheets." According to the study, the truth is that it is "in marriage . . . where the highest rates of physical satisfaction were reported."

John H. Gagnon, a professor of sociology at the State University of New York at Stony Brook, is also quoted in this article: "The marriage effect (in sexual satisfaction) is so dramatic that it swamps all other aspects of our data." Very interesting. The "experts" are discovering what God has been telling us all along—that sex in a "one-flesh" relationship is so much more fulfilling than any experience outside His design that there is no comparison.

Still wonder if God understands romance? Listen to this love poem:

"How beautiful your sandaled feet,
O prince's daughter!
Your graceful legs are like jewels,
the work of a craftsman's hands.
Your navel is a rounded goblet
that never lacks blended wine.
Your waist is a mound of wheat
encircled by lilies.
Your breasts are like two fawns,
twins of a gazelle.
Your neck is like an ivory tower.
Your eyes are the pools of Heshbon
by the gate of Bath Rabbim.
Your nose is like the tower of Lebanon
looking toward Damascus.
Your head crowns you like Mount Carmel.
Your hair is like royal tapestry;
the king is held captive by its tresses.
How beautiful you are and how pleasing,
O love, with your delights!
Your stature is like that of the palm,
and your breasts like clusters of fruit.
I said, "I will climb the palm tree;
I will take hold of its fruit."
May your breasts be like the clusters of the vine,
the fragrance of your breath like apples,
and your mouth like the best wine.

"May the wine go straight to my lover,
flowing gently over lips and teeth.
I belong to my lover,
and his desire is for me" (Song of Solomon 7:1–10).

Wow! Is it hot in here, or what! Would you want to guess who wrote that poem? Well, Solomon may have written the words, but God inspired them. There should be no further doubt that He knows all about romance and sensual love.

Sex is beautiful and God-honoring when it is experienced within His plan. Do not allow the perversion of sexuality to make you think it is an evil thing. There is nothing to be embarrassed about. Sex may be a very private matter, but godly married people are encouraged to enjoy this wonderful gift. It's a treasure to be enjoyed and cherished.

True Value

Imagine you had a Honus Wagner baseball card in your collection. Many believe this to be the most valuable baseball card in the world. It's worth thousands of dollars. You put the card on your desk and leave the house for a while. When you get home, you are greeted by the neighborhood kids riding around outside on their bikes and trikes.

The reason people abuse sexuality is not because they value it so much but because they do not value it at all.

You go inside and find, to your horror, that the Honus Wagner card is missing from your collection. You search frantically, but you can't find it anywhere. Then it dawns on you. You hope you are wrong, but it's worth a look.

Your heart in your throat, you go out to see what is making that whirring noise on the neighborhood trikes and bikes.

Sure enough, it's your worst nightmare! You discover that the kids have taken your baseball card collection and clothespinned the cards to the spokes of their bikes to make a motor noise. Even Honus Wagner has been subjected to this merciless slapping all around the neighborhood.

Poor Honus! (What kind of name is Honus, anyway?) Talk about turning the other cheek!

Like that valued card, our sexuality is a treasure to be protected. Just because others take this precious gift from God and diminish it is no reason for you to do likewise. The reason people abuse sexuality is not because they value it so much but because they do not value it at all. They are ignorant of its great worth.

Like the neighborhood kids who didn't understand the value of the Honus Wagner baseball card, ignorance of the value of your sexuality could lead to abuse or misuse. Your sexuality is a priceless gift. But be aware of the high price of misusing that gift.

Chapter 11
How to Have Lasting Sexual Fulfillment

"The Incredible Secret to Sexual Fulfillment." "Fifty Ways to Love Your Lover." "The Key to Sexual Pleasure." You've seen or heard such phrases pitched by hosts on those tacky talk shows or emblazoned across the tabloids at the grocery store.

So what is the secret to sexual fulfillment? Everyone wants to know. And, judging from the volume of information available, quite a few think they have the answer. In fact, I get a little sick just thinking about all the lives those misguided writers destroy with their suggestions on techniques and sex toys. Empty promises.

Yet plenty of readers and viewers are clamoring for such material. Why? Because their love lives are still unfulfilled. People who have found answers don't keep searching for more answers. We search because we are convinced that there must be something more, and the relentless pursuit of sexual satisfaction as a culture is a glaring admission that we haven't found it.

The relentless pursuit of sexual satisfaction as a culture is a glaring admission that we haven't found it.

According to the April 26, 1993, issue of *Newsweek* magazine, Wilt Chamberlain claimed "to have packed into his career the equivalent of 400 years of lovemaking by ordinary mortals." Why would a man be driven to such behavior if there were not a void in his life he was trying to fill? Satisfied men don't act like that. His behavior was more desperate than heroic—conclusive proof that what he had found did not satisfy.

Answers

"OK, Mister Big Shot," you might counter, "how did you become such a sex expert?" Please, the last thing I am is an expert on sex. Nor am I a psychologist or sex therapist. I'm a preacher, though some may disagree. I make my living studying the Bible and applying its truth to life. It's in the pages of God's Word that the secret to sexual fulfillment is found. The key to sex is not physical or psychological, but theological.

"Only a preacher would say a thing like that!" you argue. But it's true. Certainly sexual fulfillment reached its peak in the Garden of Eden. Adam and Eve had no hang-ups. No insecurities. No comparisons or self-esteem problems. No distortions about sex from abuse or the media. It was perfection. It was paradise! It was almost too good to be true.

Say It Ain't So

One doesn't have long to imagine Adam and Eve, hand in hand, strolling into the sunset. Their bliss was short-lived. By the third chapter of Genesis, one of the saddest chapters in the Bible, we are reading about paradise lost:

"When the woman saw that the fruit of the tree was good for food and pleasing to the eye, and also desirable for gaining wisdom, she took some and ate it. She also gave some to her husband, who was with her, and he ate it. Then the eyes of both of them were opened, and they realized they were naked; so they sewed fig leaves together and made coverings for themselves.

"Then the man and his wife heard the sound of the LORD God as he was walking in the garden in the cool of the day, and they hid" (Gen. 3:6–8).

Immediately after Adam and Eve sinned, they realized their own nakedness and scrambled for cover. Bring out the fig leaves!

You know the rest of the story. When God confronted them, they blamed each other. The first marital spat. What happened to Adam and

Eve, the perfect couple? The couple voted most likely to succeed? They had it all, but it was slipping away. They went from naked with no shame to hiding and blame.

In the very next chapter of Genesis, we are introduced to Lamech, who had two wives. What happened to two becoming one flesh? What happened to one man and one woman? How could things get this messed up in only four chapters? That's like being out of the game in the first quarter.

Desperate Behaviors

Separated from God, sexuality fell victim to the chaos brought on by sin. From being an expression of fulfillment in God to becoming a pursuit of one's own god. From a celebration before God with no shame to hiding from God because of shame. Once the fellowship with God was broken, there was an emptiness inside that could not be filled with pleasures like sex.

Solomon had all the wine, women, and song a man could ever desire. He lived a fantasy life if ever there was one. Yet listen to his conclusion to his pursuit of pleasure:

"I thought in my heart, 'Come now, I will test you with pleasure to find out what is good.' But that also proved to be meaningless. . . . I denied myself nothing my eyes desired; I refused my heart no pleasure. . . . Yet . . . everything was meaningless, a chasing after the wind; nothing was gained under the sun" (Eccl. 2:1, 10–11).

Solomon gave it his best shot and came up empty.

Paradise Regained

Can you imagine standing before your spouse and God, naked and feeling no sense of shame? As you read these words, you may not think this is possible, but it is. I guarantee it. Let me rephrase that: *God* guarantees it. Sex and shame do not have to go together.

To experience what Adam and Eve experienced before their fall, you must first be right with God. Shame entered into the picture because of disobedience. Their relationship with each other fell apart when their relationship with God was broken. Therefore, this relationship with God must be restored. Step one on the road back to paradise.

Until you are right with God, you can't do anything about your shame problem. Guilt is not an emotion you can turn on and off like a garden hose. You feel shame because you *are* shameful. Apart from God, we are all shameful. "All have sinned and fall short of the glory of God" (Rom. 3:23).

When the serpent came to Adam and Eve in the Garden of Eden, he told them that they could be like God and rewrite the Rulebook. "God knows that when you eat of it [the forbidden fruit] your eyes will be opened, and you will be like God, knowing good and evil" (Gen. 3:5). He also tried to convince the first couple that there would be no conse-quences to their choices. "'You will not surely die,' the serpent said to the woman" (v. 4). Wrong again. Adam and Eve lost it all because of their disobedience. God has written the rules, and there are consequences for those who break them. One of those consequences is shame.

Rather than trying to deny or minimize your shame, you need to address what makes you shameful. And what makes you shameful is your disobedience to God. Your failure to meet God's standard of holi-ness that identifies you as a sinner. Your determination to do things your way instead of God's way. Like Adam and Eve in the Garden, you feel ashamed because you have violated God's holiness.

So what now? Be a better person? Go to church? Do good deeds? Do more good stuff than bad? What is the remedy for this sin problem we are all plagued with? How do you find relief from the guilt and shame you feel?

Begin Here

There is only one remedy for sin and that is Jesus Christ. Jesus paid a debt He did not owe because you owed a debt you could not pay. The Bible says that the wages—what you earned because of your sin—is death. *Eternal* death. Separation from God and all the joys of heaven *for-ever.* "For the wages of sin is death . . .

" . . . but [good news!] the gift of God is eternal life in Christ Jesus our Lord" (Rom. 6:23). Jesus died in your place. He took your punishment upon Himself on the cross nearly two thousand years ago. It was His gift to you.

With that gift of salvation from sin also comes the gift of a restored relationship with Him. The gift of standing before Him without shame. Not because you've never sinned, but because your sin has been covered by His blood.

The Bible states that when you trust Jesus as your Savior, you are redeemed. To redeem something is to buy it back. The term *redemption* comes from the first-century slave market. To redeem a slave was to purchase him off the auction block and set him free. Jesus longs to purchase you from the slave market of sin and set you free. Sin brings bondage, but there is freedom from the shackles of sin if you are willing to trust Jesus as your Redeemer.

Until you are right with God, sex can never fulfill its proper role in your life.

What does all this have to do with sexuality? Everything! Until you are right with God, sex can never fulfill its proper role in your life. You cannot express fulfillment if you aren't fulfilled. You cannot be satisfied sexually if you are not satisfied in God. Remember, love and fulfillment are *expressed* in sex, not *generated* in sex. For sex to become an expression of love and fulfillment, you must first experience love and fulfillment in God.

Adam and Eve were not searching for anything or needing anything when they experienced sexuality in the Garden. They were perfect beings, expressing their satisfaction in God to each other. Their relationship with each other simply flowed out of their relationship with Him.

You, too, can have a relationship with God through Jesus Christ. At last, your weary soul can be satisfied. You can have what you have been pursuing in all the wrong places.

From Disappointment to Delight

Ultimately, a lack of sexual fulfillment is not a physical problem but a spiritual one. No amount of tutoring on sexual techniques can compensate for spiritual emptiness. Sex as god has no ability to satisfy; it's an impotent idol. Ignore God, and sex will never be all it's meant to be.

Many people, even in marriage relationships, are disappointed to find that sexuality is not what they had hoped. They had always believed that if they met the right person, fell in love, and got married, they would live happily ever after. They believed their partner would satisfy the emptiness in their soul. Now they wonder why the emptiness remains after

months or years of sex with their marriage partner. They want to do the right thing, but they are still not satisfied. What's missing?

> *For sex to be an expression of fulfillment and love,*
> *you need to be sourced in God.*

Some believe they aren't satisfied because their partner isn't a good enough lover. "If she (or he) was just better in bed," they argue with themselves. Some then turn to extramarital affairs or pornography or other perversions to meet their needs. Yet no matter what they try, they remain empty and unfulfilled.

What we ultimately need, a marriage partner cannot produce. The apostle John said that only those who know God can truly know love. "Dear friends, let us love one another, for love comes from God. Everyone who loves has been born of God and knows God. Whoever does not love does not know God, because God is love" (1 John 4:7–8). For sex to be an expression of fulfillment and love, you need to be sourced in God.

Most people think God will limit sexual pleasure. I would suggest it's just the opposite. In Him we find ultimate pleasure. "Delight yourself in the LORD and he will give you the desires of your heart" (Ps. 37:4). To "delight" means to take great pleasure in. Or this gem: "You have made known to me the path of life; you will fill me with joy in your presence, with eternal pleasures at your right hand" (16:11). With God, we experience pleasure not for a season, but forever. Not a temporary thrill, but pleasure that lasts.

What you're pursuing in a sexual relationship is ultimately a hunger for a relationship with God. Sex between a husband and wife is still, at best, only a taste of the pleasure we can experience in Him. The teenager becoming sexually active, the woman cheating on her husband, the businessman chasing solitary one-night stands—all these are signs of a deep need for the divine.

They may not know it, but their souls will continue to starve, remain unsatisfied, until they have tasted the Bread of Life, Jesus Christ. He is also the only One who can quench our thirst.

Thirsty No More

She had come to fetch her daily supply of water when the sun was at its zenith. Better the long, hot trek to the well when the other women were at home in the heat of the day than to face their crude comments. Always when they gathered, their conversation was of husbands and children and the dull drudgery of their lives. Except when she was present— then, they spoke of her, snickering behind their hands.

She is the loose woman who can't keep a man happy. She has had five—count them—five husbands! She is an embarrassment to the whole village.

Her dreams were like those of any woman. A longing for love, a home, family. Someone to care for her and help carry the load. Thinking of it now, she realized that none of her husbands had given her what she yearned for. By the fourth and fifth husband, her expectations were more practical than passionate.

Man number six she didn't even bother to marry. He was there to help her make it through another day—and endless nights. Both of them, outcasts of society. Loneliness crept over her like an evening chill. Would life always be like this?

He made her nervous and uncomfortable, but His eyes were filled with a compassion she'd never seen before.

At the well she was joined by a Jewish traveler. Strange. Not many Jews traveled through Samaria. The Jews and Samaritans despised one another. Most Jews, the devout ones anyway, would take the longer route rather than risk being contaminated on Samaritan soil.

"Let me have a drink," the Stranger asked. How odd. Jewish men did not speak to Samaritan women. When she asked about it, she expected a simple answer, if she got an answer at all. But she wasn't prepared for Him to speak in riddles and to answer her question with a question. And what was this about "living water"?

It made sense. "Anyone who drinks today will be thirsty tomorrow," He said. Yet those who would drink of this "living water" would never thirst again. Really? If that were true, it would save her many a trip to the well.

Then, just as she was relaxing a bit with Him, the man said something entirely unexpected. He told her to invite her husband to join them. Embarrassed and hoping to avoid further discussion, she mumbled that she didn't have a husband.

Like a bolt of lightning, His next words shattered all composure, for He told her that she had spoken truly, since she was now living with a sixth man who was not her husband. Surely this Man was a prophet, since He seemed to know everything about her!

Wide-eyed, she listened to every word He uttered, soaking up His life-giving message like a thirsty sponge. And when He revealed His identity—that He was the long-awaited Messiah, the Anointed One sent from God—she believed. She had gone down the hill to fetch water for the day and had met a Man who could see deep into her heart, who knew her as no other man had ever known her.

For the first time in years, hope coursed through her body. Somehow she knew she had found what the six men in her life could not deliver. She had found real love, meaning, and purpose with the Lover of her soul.

Please understand, you do not come to Jesus to improve your sex life. You come to Jesus because you desperately need a Savior. You come to Jesus to be reconciled to the God who created you and loves you. Having found Him, you are then able to put the other pieces of your life in order, including your sexuality.

Parable of the Gardener and the Flower

✝

Parable of the Gardener and the Flower

†

The dying seedling knew she had made the wrong choice. The hot sun, the wind, the lack of water and care were all taking their toll. Her leaves were brown and limp, her head bowed in surrender to the elements.

She could see the gardener in the distance, caring for his prized flowers. The blossoms, flamboyantly colorful, stood straight and tall, basking in the sun and drinking in the morning showers.

When the little flower was a seed, she had been part of them. She had known life in the garden, but wondered if there wasn't more beyond its boundaries. She would stare at the open fields, longing for her freedom. The wild flowers were free to do as they pleased. Out in the field, there was no gardener in charge.

In the garden, the flowers were subjected to daily routines of watering and weeding and pruning. Pruning was painful. The wild flowers had no such worries. They didn't have to fuss over a few harmless weeds, and they certainly didn't need to be pruned. They were left to grow wherever they wished, and that's just what the little seed desired.

The other flowers tried to warn the seedling of the dangers out in the fields, but she wouldn't listen. So, one windy day, she just let go and allowed the wind to carry her aloft. What a ride! For the first time in her life, she felt free. She dreamed of where she might land and what pleasures awaited her there.

She landed, rather abruptly, in a lush field. The young flower thought this the most beautiful place she had ever seen. No boundaries, no limits, no gardeners. Surely it must be paradise.

But as she began to sprout, she noticed that the grass seemed greener on the other side of the field. She was also surprised at how painful it was to put down roots. The soil seemed to be filled with rocks and broken glass and other sharp objects that tore at her tender shoots. Still, it was better than the flower garden.

Her neighborhood grew rapidly, but most of her new neighbors were from that pesky weed family. Some looked nice enough until you got to know them and found out they were really quite annoying. They wanted everything their way. They hogged all the water and food and took more than their fair share of the dirt. Some were real bullies. When they started pushing the young flower around, she began to think that maybe the garden plot wasn't so bad after all. She tried to bloom and pretend she was happy, but eventually her weedy neighbors won out and pushed her aside.

In the distance she could see the flower garden, and every day she would watch the gardener tenderly caring for his flowers. Oh, to be back in the garden again! Her freedom had turned out to be bondage, and the wild flowers, nothing but weeds. If only she had seen the field so clearly from the flower garden. But alas, she had not.

When it seemed all hope was gone, the hard earth beneath her began to move. She was lifted into the air in a pile of dirt and transported across the field. Coming to a landing next to the flower garden, she looked into the faces of the majestic flowers. They had been right. They had tried to warn her. Now just look at her!

She expected to find "I-told-you-so" expressions in their faces. Rather, they looked at her with tender compassion. "Welcome home, little flower," they said, nodding in greeting.

The gardener reached down and gently pulled the little flower from the weeds and rocks and broken glass. He brushed the dirt from her wilted leaves and carefully planted her in the flower garden. Then the gardener lifted her head, which hung low in shame, and bound it to the strong stem of another flower. In this way she could see the sun and drink in the morning rains until she was able to stand on her own again.

Who would have thought! The gardener had seen her, neglected and wilting among the weeds, and rescued her in spite of her foolish choices. He had picked her up, graciously cleaned her up, and replanted her in the very garden she had once rejected. In the following days, she found that all of the flowers that stood so proudly here were transplants from other sad places.

Under his care, the little flower was soon blooming happily, yielding to the occasional pinching and pruning, grateful for the refreshing drink of water the gardener gave her from his watering can and the warmth of the sun on her bruised leaves. *Yes*, she thought, *I think I know now why all the flowers here are so bright and beautiful. It is their way of showing gratitude to the one who loved us, saved us, and allowed us to bloom again!*

Chapter 12
Midnight in the Garden

Gethsemane. Another garden. Not paradise, but a place of pain so intense that He was sweating blood. "My soul is overwhelmed with sorrow to the point of death," He told His friends as He left them to keep watch while He prayed.

Moving to a more solitary spot in the olive garden, He fell on His knees and began to pour out His heart. "*Abba*, Father; everything is possible for you. Take this cup from me. Yet not what I will, but what you will" (Mark 14:34, 36).

But His friends fell asleep on the job. Peter, James, and John—Jesus' most trusted disciples. When He returned to find them sleeping, He said, "Could you not keep watch for one hour? Watch and pray so that you will not fall into temptation. The spirit is willing, but the body is weak" (vv. 37–38).

Jesus knew all about temptation. During His life on earth, He was the target of Satan's most devious schemes. But Satan hadn't been able to buy Him off. Not with the promise of satisfaction for His fleshly appetites. Not with the prospect of taking an easy route to ministry. Not with the possibility of possessing all the kingdoms of the world.

Maybe it was not too late, Satan was surely thinking. The great Creator God of the universe in human flesh should not have to suffer the cruelest death ever conceived, death by crucifixion, for the sins of those idiots He had made! Why even His own closest friends didn't appreciate Him enough to stay awake when He needed them most.

How interesting that in this moment of agony, Jesus should be thinking of them—of our welfare. Warning us of the dangers of temptation. He knew it would be tough for us. Just because He was God's Son, He was not exempt from suffering. He *chose* to feel what we feel. "For we do not have a high priest who is unable to sympathize with our weaknesses, but we have one who has been tempted in every way, just as we are—yet was without sin" (Heb. 4:15). Incredible!

Baiting the Hook

One early spring day, a friend of mine and I decided to do some fishing in a pond near our home. Because the fish are still in their winter pattern, early spring fishing can be slow. Sure enough, we fished for a couple of hours with no luck.

At that point I made a strategic move. I knew that the water was fairly deep under a big, old log about twenty feet from the bank, and if the fish were in their winter pattern, they'd most likely be in deep water. Having carefully made my assessment, with careful precision, I threw my plastic worm around that tree again and again. Maybe if I irritated the fish, I could provoke them to attack the bait out of anger, even if they weren't hungry.

I cast my line in the same spot for well over an hour. Still no luck. From all indications, there were no fish in the lake at all. Then it happened. Without any warning I saw the slightest twitch in my line. That twitch was more than I had seen all day, so I reared back and set the hook. To my amazement a huge, largemouth bass came thrashing out of the water. I've got proof how big he was. Come by my office someday, and you can see for yourself. He's mounted on my wall.

Temptation, like fishing, is the art of deception.

The strategy of fishing is based on the art of deception. My job as a fisherman is to make the fish think that a piece of plastic with a hook in it is really lunch on a line. The fish thinks he is getting a snack, but all he is going to get is a face full of hook. You have to deceive fish to catch fish. That's the art of fishing.

The Bible uses fishing as a picture of temptation. Often, when speaking on the subject, the New Testament writers used a word that means "to bait a hook or bait a trap." For example, James wrote, "But each one is tempted when, by his own evil desire, he is dragged away and *enticed*" (1:14). Temptation, like fishing, is the art of deception—being enticed.

Never Say Never

Oh, it couldn't happen to me, you say. I've been around the block a time or two.

I wouldn't be so sure, if I were you. If the great King David could fall, so can you. The polls indicate that 80 percent of Americans believe adultery is wrong, yet people have affairs every day. Just knowing what is right is not enough. It takes a game plan.

Careless thinking is the first step toward destruction.

Those of you who think it could never happen to you are the most vulnerable. Your carelessness can cause you to be unprepared when temptation comes. And it will. Like that unsuspecting fish, you can be lured and hooked before you know it. You may find yourself doing the very thing you never thought you'd do.

Some of you, as you read this book, are in what I call the "red zone." You are allowing thoughts to enter your mind that should not be there. You are entertaining sexual fantasies that are dishonoring to God. You are starting to rationalize thoughts and behavior because you think they will bring pleasure and satisfaction. This is your wake-up call, friends. Warning! Warning!

For some of you, temptation is fueled by being around certain people. For others, it's filling your mind with images from racy videos, television, or magazines. No one just happens to give in to temptation one day. It's a process that begins in the mind.

Careless thinking is the first step toward destruction. And you who think you have nothing to worry about are at the highest risk of all to take a fall.

Game Face

Athletes talk about getting their "game faces" on. This means they are focused and ready to do battle. They are not distracted by other things, but are committed to putting their full energies into preparing for the contest ahead. They understand the strategy and their assignment and are ready to give it their best shot.

Once you have acknowledged your vulnerability in the area of sexuality, put on your game face. Review your strategy and prepare to do battle with the opposition. No excuses. No blaming past problems or present circumstances. Only a fierce determination to do God's will.

What is His will? Paul gives it to us straight: "It is God's will that you should be sanctified [set apart, different from the others]; that you should avoid sexual immorality" (1 Thess. 4:3). One of the young ladies in the *Prime Time Live* special stated, "I never thought what I was doing was wrong—because it never comes right out and says that pre-marital sex is wrong in the Bible." I'm not sure what Bible she reads, but there is no doubt how God feels about sex outside of marriage. It is God's will that we remain pure.

Do not be deceived. Temptation promises what it cannot deliver. Like the fish, you will think you are getting what you want and end up with a face full of hook. Sex was not designed by God to fill the void in your life. You are being duped if you think you'll find what you're looking for in a sexual experience.

God sees things much more clearly than you do. He sees the big picture. The deception of the enemy. The destruction that will follow. Better listen to God's warnings. He's extremely specific: Anything outside of His design and purpose cannot and will not satisfy. You can take that one to the bank.

"Nip It in the Bud"

The old *Andy Griffith Show* featured one of my favorite characters of all time, Barney Fife. Barney was a gun-slingin', tough-as-nails, worldly wise deputy sheriff who patrolled the streets of Mayberry, RFD. Actually, he was more like a kid playing dress-up in a cop's uniform. But don't burst my bubble; he's my hero.

When things seemed like they were getting out of hand, Barney would advise his pal Andy that they "nip it in the bud." That meant put a stop to it early "before there's real trouble"—like jaywalking in Mayberry. What a sorry day *that* would be.

Once you have conceded your vulnerability and put your game face on, you need to understand the nature and process of temptation. You've got to nip it in the bud.

The nature of temptation is an enticement to meet a legitimate need through illegitimate means. Wanting to feel loved and cared for, satisfied and fulfilled are legitimate needs. Wanting to experience the pleasure of a sexual relationship is a legitimate desire.

But trying to meet legitimate needs and desires through illegitimate means is wrong. An illegitimate "means" sexually is anything that is outside of God's design or purpose. It's black and white. Any attempt to meet a sexual need apart from a "one-flesh" marriage relationship is sin. God's guidelines on this topic are very clear.

Temptation starts in the mind. It starts with thinking that is not in alignment with God's truth. No one gets up one morning and says, "I believe I'll go out today and ruin my life." But it happens! It happens because people are deceived into thinking something that isn't true. They think that certain behaviors will meet legitimate needs in their lives. They think a sexual relationship will make them feel loved and special. They think the plastic worm will satisfy their hungry belly. In the end they get a face full of hook. To nip it in the bud, we must never entertain thoughts we know are untrue. If our thinking is right our behavior will be right. Our thought life is where we win or lose the battle.

Stillborn

Once your thinking is messed up, the result will be deception. Let's check in with James again. This practical apostle has more to say on the subject of temptation: "Each one is tempted when, by his own evil desire, he is dragged away and enticed. Then, after desire [wrong thoughts] has conceived, it gives birth to sin; and sin, when it is full-grown, gives birth to death" (1:14–15).

The phrase for "gives birth to death" means to be "stillborn." In this passage, James is using the imagery of the conception, growth, and birth of a baby. The baby, which is sin, is conceived in the mind. As deceptive thoughts are entertained (pondered, nurtured, fed with sexual images, etc.), the "baby" grows. When these thoughts come to term, the baby is born, but there is no life. No life means no fulfillment. What you thought would bring so much pleasure has brought only heartache. The behavior that in the womb [the mind] promised satisfaction has delivered grief.

It's a mind thing. "Therefore, prepare your *minds* for action; be self-controlled; set your hope fully on the grace to be given you when Jesus Christ is revealed" (1 Pet. 1:13). You are to battle sexual temptation in your mind, not your emotions. Rather than trying to abort a baby that has already been conceived and has grown to full-term, we must avoid conception in the first place. Thinking correctly about sexuality is the key to victory and purity. You need to put your game face on and prepare to do battle in your mind.

To avoid repeating old patterns, it would be wise to know what we're up against. I should say *whom* we're up against. The opposition is fierce. The face of evil is not a pretty sight.

Personal Enemy #1

"Your enemy the devil prowls around like a roaring lion looking for someone to devour," Peter warns (1 Pet. 5:8). Satan makes his living trying to deceive those who will listen to him. He delights in enticing his prey to take the bait, only to set the hook and watch death move in.

Peter described our enemy as a roaring lion. But Annie Dillard, in her classic *Pilgrim at Tinker's Creek*, thinks he looks more like a giant water bug:

"A couple of summers ago I was walking along the edge of the island to see what I could see in the water, and mainly to scare frogs. . . . At the end of the island I noticed a small green frog. He was exactly half in and half out of the water.

"He didn't jump: I crept closer. At last I knelt on the island's winter-killed grass, lost, dumbstruck, staring at the frog in the creek just four feet away. He was a very small frog with wide, dull eyes. And just as I looked at him, he slowly crumpled and began to sag. The spirit vanished from his eyes as if snuffed. His skin emptied and drooped; his very skull seemed to collapse and settle like a kicked tent.

"He was shrinking before my very eyes like a deflating football. I watched the taut, glistening skin on his shoulders ruck, rumple, and fall. Soon, part of his skin, formless as a pricked balloon, lay in floating folds like bright scum on top of the water; it was a monstrous and terrible thing. . . . An oval shadow hung in the water behind the drained frog; then the shadow glided away. The frog skin bag started to sink.

"I had read about the water bug, but never seen one. 'Giant water bug' is really the name of the creature, which is an enormous, heavy-bodied brown beetle. It eats insects, tadpoles, fish and frogs. Its grasping forelegs are mighty and hooked inward. It seizes a victim with these legs, hugs it tight and paralyzes it with the enzymes injected during a vicious bite. That one bite is the only bite it ever takes. Through the puncture shoots the poison that dissolves the victim's muscles and bones and organs—all but the skin—and through it the giant water bug sucks out the victim's body, reduced to a juice."

I believe that's an apt description of the foe we face in the battle for sexual purity. Get ready. He plays dirty.

Prepare to Fight

Those who desire to walk in purity before God need to realize that this world is not a playground; it's a battleground.

There has never been a generation in the history of the world that has been as bombarded with as much sexual information and stimulation as this one. A recent CNN/*Time* poll reveals the fact that of teens between the ages of thirteen and seventeen, 82 percent have used the Internet. Of these, 44 percent have viewed sites with information on sex. *USA Today* reported that Americans spent $8 billion to $12 billion in 1996 on pornographic videos, magazines, and phone sex. Sex is everywhere! It's only a matter of time—like seconds—before you're the next target.

While a college student, I lived on the fourth floor of the men's dorm. Our arch rivals lived on the seventeenth floor. One winter night we had so much snow they canceled school the next day. This meant we had all night to play.

After careful deliberation, we decided to initiate an indoor snowball fight with the seventeenth floor. We sneaked out the fire door, filled trash cans with snow, and prepared our arsenal. To hide our identity, we all put on our ski masks and headed up to meet the adversary.

Our unsuspecting victims were sitting around the lounge in various stages of dress—and *un*dress. On the signal we crashed the party and launched our arsenal of snow-packed "bullets" in their direction. They were screaming and diving for cover, unable to escape our frosty assault.

Once we had exhausted our supply of snowballs, we quickly escaped back down the stairs to the safety of our own floor.

Get ready for the attack. Don't be caught off guard.

"What do we do now?" someone asked. After considering our options, we selected the plan most appropriate to our situation. We decided to attack again. We refilled the cans and headed for the seventeenth floor again.

This time the guys were all gathered around a table in the lounge, making plans to mount a counterattack. Without warning, we burst in again and buried them in a second volley of snowballs.

What was the key to our resounding victory? We were prepared to fight and they were not. They were caught unsuspecting. Had they known we were coming, the outcome could have been very different. This is what Peter had in mind by "prepare your minds." Get ready. Don't be caught off guard. Don't fall asleep on the job. Put your game face on. Without question, this is an area where you will have to constantly do battle.

We must understand that if we don't engage our minds, we cannot fight the enemy. Your belief system is to spiritual battle what a scud missile was to the Gulf War. If we choose to think with our feelings (or our hormones), we are asking for trouble. We've got to get serious about this vital area of our lives.

How do you prepare your mind? Fill it with truth. Where do you find the truth about sex? Not from books by Dr. Ruth or the latest sex manuals. You find the real truth about sexuality in the Bible. This book has been an attempt to dig out and explain God's Word about sex to equip you to win. If the truth isn't clear, reread it, think about it, process it. Do what you have to do to get it into your head before you get caught unprepared and have to pay the price. That price will be more than a snowball on a cold winter's night or a face full of hook. It could mean a lifetime of misery.

Chapter 13
For Singles Only:
How Far Is Too Far?

Remember Angie? She was carrying a load of baggage from her dysfunctional past that set her up for disaster. But it didn't help any that she wasn't mentally prepared for temptation when it came. She played with fire, not expecting to get burned. Wrong.

One of the questions that most single people wrestle with is: How far can I go physically before it is too far? Good question. No easy answer.

Some want to make this a black-and-white issue by coming up with a formula that applies to everyone. For example, no hand holding! No kissing! Or no kissing to exceed three seconds! This often becomes more of a form of legalism than a God-honoring standard. Just another kind of bondage. So what do we do?

The first step is to examine your motives. Why are you asking that question in the first place? Are you wanting to know where the line is so you can push it to the limit without stepping over? If so, you're missing the whole point of relationship.

As believers, our goal should be to be like Christ, to cultivate character that reflects the presence of God in our lives. If this is true, then our motivation should be about pleasing Him rather than hanging out near "the line." The popular slogan "What Would Jesus Do?" is a good question to ask yourself. One thing He *didn't* do when He walked this earth was to walk a tightrope between what is acceptable and unacceptable behavior. Jesus didn't live by the standard; He *is* the Standard.

Power Source

God didn't leave us on our own to become like Jesus. He didn't leave us to our best guess for WWJD. He sent an Ally, a Helper, a Guide, and Counselor—the Holy Spirit—to dwell in us and empower us to live the life. Every believer in Christ has His Spirit living on the inside (Rom. 8:9). He's the Power Source.

But how do we turn on the power? It begins with prayer. Ask, "God, how can I honor You in this relationship and, in the process, honor the person I'm with?" God really enjoys answering this kind of prayer. He may use the counsel of parents, pastors, peers, or even a book like this as part of the answer. More often, as the Author of the Best-seller of all time, he will use His own Word. Check out the Book of Proverbs, especially chapters 5–7. It doesn't get any plainer than this:

"[Keep yourself] from the immoral woman [or man]....Do not lust in your heart after her beauty or let her captivate you with her eyes ....

"Can a man [or woman] scoop fire into his lap without his clothes being burned? Can a man walk on hot coals without his feet being scorched?... But a man who commits adultery [or fornication] lacks judgment; whoever does so destroys himself" (6:24–25, 27–28, 32).

You need to read these chapters for yourself. With the Holy Spirit as your guide, I can guarantee that if you're really "hearing" these words, something will jump off the page, tailor-made for your situation. If that happens, you can know for sure that the Spirit is guiding you "into all truth."

Would I do what I'm doing with my partner in front of Jesus?

Your body, your earthly "house," is "the temple of the Holy Spirit . . . you are not your own" (1 Cor. 6:19). With the Spirit as your permanent houseguest, every time you go out with someone, you take Him with you. You can't leave Him at home. You can't ditch Him when you don't want Him around. He's involved in whatever behavior you choose to engage in with your partner. Better ask, *Would I do what I'm doing with her [him] in front of Jesus?* Believe me, you do whatever you do in front of Him every day. Sobering thought.

How Much Is Too Much?

OK. Let's get down to the nitty-gritty. As a single person, what can you do that honors God and doesn't cheapen your relationship with a person you admire?

You really want to know? Try First Corinthians 7:1 for starters: "It is good for a man not to touch a woman" (NKJV).

"Oh, great!" you say. "I knew it! You might as well lock me in the closet until my wedding day!"

In this verse, Paul was clearly speaking about what kind of touch is appropriate for unmarried couples. But hold on. Let's understand what he was really saying. The word *touch* means "to light the fire of passion." In other words, don't touch someone in a way that will ignite a passion that is only meant to be satisfied in a full sexual expression.

God has wired the human body in such a way that when the fire of passion is lit, our bodies release chemicals intended to make the experience pleasurable and powerful. God never intended for that process to be started, then stuffed. So . . . the conclusion is only logical: Don't start the engine if you can't finish the race.

What lights the fire differs with different people, based on personality, past experience, current needs, etc. That's why a rigid legalistic code of behavior won't work. God didn't cut us out with a cookie cutter. For those who have been sexually active or have viewed sexually explicit materials, their fuse will be very short. Others who have maintained purity may have a slightly longer fuse because they don't have all the baggage. If you don't know when you go from a meaningful touch to lighting the fire of passion, I would say you aren't mature enough to be going out in the first place. This isn't rocket science, friends. It's not that difficult to discern the line when we have committed this matter to God in prayer and are genuinely seeking to honor Him in our behavior.

Don't start the engine if you can't finish the race.

We've said it before. We'll say it again. If you are feasting on highly volatile material in magazines, movies, television, music, or the Internet, you're starting your engine and racing down the track, only to have to slam on the brakes before the finish line. Don't do it! Save it for the real thing. It's worth the wait. I promise.

True Love Waits

Even in this sexually saturated culture, it is possible to walk in purity before God. I know some single people who managed to do just that. Take Todd and Rose, for example. I'll let them tell this love story in their own words:

Todd: After accepting Christ at fifteen, I became part of a great youth group, where I learned what the Bible has to say about sex—what a gift it is and how God planned it for one man and one woman. I decided to make a commitment to wait until marriage.

Rose: I grew up in a home and church that taught me to wait until marriage to have sex. I didn't really understand all the reasons why until I began to see some of my friends struggling with the issue. Those who chose to have sex because it was "fun" began to flounder in their relationships, and one friend even became pregnant. The decisions she was forced to make because she had given in let me know that a little "fun" isn't worth the risk.

Todd: Even as a teenager I began to pray for my future wife. I hoped that wherever she was, she loved the Lord and was learning to walk with Him.

Rose: Like most girls, I dreamed of getting married someday and prayed that God would bring into my life someone who felt the way I did. I had heard that people who have sex before marriage sometimes carry feelings from other relationships over into marriage and compare his or her mate with a previous lover. I didn't want that to happen to me! I wanted to be the only one my husband had ever slept with.

Todd: I dated a little in high school, but tended to spend most of my free time in learning the disciplines of Bible study, prayer, fellowship, and service to Christ through short-term mission trips and camp experiences. Not to say that I was any different from any other normal guy. Sure, I had desires and feelings. But God is pretty specific about sexual activity outside marriage. So I waited—and stayed busy.

Rose: I didn't date much in high school. My crowd did things together.

I didn't want to risk being tempted sexually, so I didn't put myself into compromising situations. If I ever was alone with a guy, it was usually a good friend who had no hidden agenda.

Todd: When I went off to college, I gave even more serious thought to the kind of woman I wanted to marry. But I had to go through a stage of first finding contentment in Christ alone. I don't believe we find our "other half" when we marry, but another "whole" person who brings a lot to the relationship. When I met Rose, I knew I had found that person.

Rose: Todd was definitely God's choice for me. A guy who believed like I did about the really important issues of life. A guy who loved God with all his heart. A man who was waiting for me just as I had been waiting for him. Five months after we met, we started going out as a couple.

Todd: Even before our first date, we prayed that God would show both of us whether this was His plan. When we felt His OK, we started dating, but kept ourselves pure until our wedding night. We got married my senior year, when I was twenty-three and she was twenty-two.

Rose: Because we waited until marriage to have sex, we don't struggle with issues of trust. Oh, we have our differences occasionally, just like any other married couple, but we've already passed one of the most important tests of a relationship. We have proven that we can be faithful to each other "as long as we both shall live." And that's a great feeling.

Enough said?

Run, Baby, Run!

What do you do when you get careless and feel yourself slipping into temptation, or perhaps you get into a situation that couldn't have been avoided? There is one last resort. Basically, this strategy is simply putting into action what everyone else—peers, parents, the Word of God, the Holy Spirit—has been saying all along.

When Joseph was tempted sexually, he literally *ran* out of the room where the seductress was weaving her nasty web (see Gen. 39). Paul endorses this strategy: "Flee from sexual immorality. All other sins a man commits are outside his body, but he who sins sexually sins against his own body" (1 Cor. 6:18). Get out! Get away! Stay out of the red zone!

If the person you're with pushes your standards beyond what is pleasing to God, get out! Get away! You can't play games with sexual sin. You may resist this person twenty times, but if you give in the twenty-first?

Well, the consequences will be just as severe. Remember Angie? Once was all it took.

Satisfy Your Soul

One final thought, which is perhaps the most important one I could share with a single person. I have mentioned it previously, but I want to highlight it here again. When those sexual urges come upon you, and they will, don't stuff those longings. For years, singles have been told to take a cold shower and say no to those sexual urges. I believe this is going against the very design of how God has made you and will only lead to frustration. Rather than trying to stuff your passions, you need to redirect them.

Ultimately what your soul is longing for when you are tempted sexually is to be intimate with God. This is why sex outside of marriage makes matters worse. Sexual sin distances you from God, making the longings all the more intense, leaving you more vulnerable to the next sexual temptation.

As a single person, you do not need to go unfulfilled. Do not resort to self-gratification. You can have your desire satisfied in God. Give your soul that for which it thirsts. When you are tempted, get alone with God. Worship privately or corporately. Open up God's Word and seek Him. Find out what draws you into a more intimate experience with God, and pursue that with all your passion when sexual temptation comes knocking at the door of your heart. You will find that rather than going away frustrated, you will go away deeper in love with Jesus.

This explains why God made us all with such strong sexual desires—so that we might passionately pursue Him and know Him intimately. What a great thing to know that no one has to live unfulfilled, whether married or single.

Chapter 14
Amazing Grace—God Really Does Forgive

"But God can't forgive me! You don't know what I've done!"

You'd be surprised how many times I've heard *that* one. It seems that when it comes to sexual sin, many folks can't get past it. They want to wallow around in it, listening to the lies of the deceiver, who sits on their shoulders whispering that this time they've gone too far. That not even God will forgive *this* sin.

Those who think Jesus gets a kick out of condemning people don't really know Him. He gave His life for your sins—*all* of them—including your sexual sin.

One woman learned that lesson well . . . .

Scarlet Woman, Scarlet Thread

She might as well be wearing a big red letter on her robe. She'd already been branded an adulteress by the religious crowd. She knew, too, that her life was in danger. Under the Mosaic Law, this offense was punishable by death. If discovered, both parties—the man and the woman—were to be killed by stoning (Deut. 22:22). But it didn't matter. Nothing mattered anymore.

She had spent last night—again—in the arms of a married man in another vain attempt to find some way to fill the gaping hole in her heart. And then they had found her—those religious people. They had caught her in the act. She had no defense. She was guilty. And now here she was, waiting for the first rock to strike her.

She braced herself, head lowered. Maybe the first would render her unconscious. She wished for that state. Anything to numb the aching emptiness, the rejection and humiliation. But the men were talking now, and someone was scratching something in the dust at her feet.

Out of the corner of her eyes, she caught a glimpse of Him. He was not one of them. This Man was Someone she had never seen before. For the first time since He had been standing there, He spoke:

"'If anyone is without sin, let him be the first to throw a stone at her.'" Again he stooped down and wrote on the ground.

"At this, those who heard began to go away one at a time, the older ones first, until only Jesus was left, with the woman still standing there. Jesus straightened up and asked her, 'Woman, where are they? Has no one condemned you?'

"'No one, sir,' she said.

"'Then neither do I condemn you,' Jesus declared. 'Go now and leave your life of sin'" (John 8:7–11).

It's obvious from the story that this woman's captors didn't care about her or her sin. Their intent was to force Jesus to make a wrong move so they could condemn Him. She was a mere pawn in their sinister plan. Like so many men in her life, they were using her to get what they wanted.

Jesus, knowing the hearts and motives of the religious leaders, chose to forgive rather than condemn. Like the gardener in the parable, He offered compassion and grace to one who deserved punishment.

Whatever your past, however shameful your behavior,
God stands ready to forgive.

Imagine the thoughts racing through the mind of this woman. She went from a death sentence to a pardon in the time it takes for a stone to drop to the ground. From condemned to forgiven. She had finally found what she had been searching for. Unconditional love. Not in the lust-filled arms of another man, but in the arms of grace.

Because of Jesus

Whatever your past, however shameful your behavior, God stands ready to forgive. You may beat yourself up over your sin, thinking He will somehow be impressed by how sorry you are. You may think that if you "pay" for your sin, God will be obligated to grant you a pardon. Not accepting His forgiveness until you've figured out some way to earn it may seem like humility, but it is actually pride.

The reality is you can't pay for your sin at all. God is not impressed when you beat yourself up. He is not impressed by your attempt to make good on your sin. To imply that you, or anyone else, could do anything to merit His forgiveness is offensive to Him. He offers forgiveness as a gift of His grace.

He sent Jesus to cut the cords binding you to your sin. Your part is to acknowledge your sin, confess it, and receive His forgiveness.

Like the woman caught in adultery, you are being offered another chance. God is not condemning you. So get on with your life and don't sin like that anymore.

The reality is you can't pay for your sin at all. God is not impressed when we beat ourselves up.

Beauty from Ashes

He sat in his chair, holding his newborn child, trying to digest the news he'd heard that day. His son—this tiny, helpless baby boy—was special to God. How did he know? Because God Himself had named the child, and the name meant "beloved of the Lord."

He should not have this son, and he knew it. More than that, he should not have been allowed to keep the boy's mother as his wife. It would have been just if the Lord had closed her womb. The memories unrolled like a scroll . . . .

She had belonged to another man when he'd first had sex with her. Adultery, plain and simple. Through that affair, she had become pregnant. To cover his sin, he'd had the woman's husband killed. As the commander-in-chief of the army, he had ordered the man to the front lines of battle. His conscience condemned him for the ten-thousandth time.

He had waited a while before marrying the woman, hoping no one would notice. How could he have been so foolish? Everyone knew. They could count the months, couldn't they?

The child conceived of their sin was born, but died in infancy—

God's judgment. How did he know? God had told him, for he was not just any man but God's chosen leader of His people—the king! He had failed miserably in his great responsibility, and he wrestled with the possibility that he would suffer the consequences of his sin for the rest of his life.

Yet now, holding in his arms this second son, borne of a wife he shouldn't have, the king realized again that God is a God of forgiveness. He didn't deserve this precious gift. Yet just today, God had foretold that the child—Jedidiah, or Solomon—would someday be great in the kingdom.

What the king could not know then was that this son would grow up to be king of Israel, a man of wisdom, and to write the most beautiful poem on romantic love in the history of literature. What irony that a boy who came from such a dysfunctional family could be used to express the beauty of sexuality in a marriage relationship. Only God could do something like that—bring such beauty from the ashes of failure.

Forgiven!

The story of David and his sin with Bathsheba is a remarkable one. Who would have thought that the great king of Israel, "a man after God's own heart," would be capable of adultery, using murder as a cover-up! Second Samuel 11 tells the story of David's sexual sin, summing up the entire affair with the words, "But the thing David had done displeased the LORD" (v. 27b). "Displeased?" This statement sounds like one for the "duh" file. Of *course* God was displeased with David. But the writer wants to make sure we understand the gravity of David's sin before he introduces us to God's response.

David, too, must have been heartsick over his failure. Unable to face the God he had offended, he tried to bury his guilt. It was only after the prophet Nathan confronted him that David's sinful heart was broken, and he came clean.

Psalm 51 records David's confession. For those of you who struggle with accepting God's forgiveness, insert your own name and read this psalm as a prayer from your heart to His:

"Have mercy on me, O God,
according to your unfailing love;
according to your great compassion
blot out my transgressions.
Wash away all my iniquity
and cleanse me from my sin.

"For I know my transgressions,
and my sin is always before me.
Against you, you only, have I sinned
and done what is evil in your sight,
so that you are proved right when you speak
and justified when you judge.
Surely I was sinful at birth,
sinful from the time my mother conceived me.
Surely you desire truth in the inner parts;
you teach me wisdom in the inmost place.

"Cleanse me with hyssop, and I will be clean;
wash me, and I will be whiter than snow.
Let me hear joy and gladness;
let the bones you have crushed rejoice.
Hide your face from my sins
and blot out all my iniquity.

"Create in me a pure heart, O God,
and renew a steadfast spirit within me.
Do not cast me from your presence
or take your Holy Spirit from me.
Restore to me the joy of your salvation
and grant me a willing spirit, to sustain me.
"Then I will teach transgressors your ways,
and sinners will turn back to you.
Save me from bloodguilt, O God,
the God who saves me,
and my tongue will sing of your righteousness.

O Lord, open my lips,
and my mouth will declare your praise.
You do not delight in sacrifice, or I would bring it;
you do not take pleasure in burnt offerings.
The sacrifices of God are a broken spirit;
a broken and contrite heart,
O God, you will not despise" (Ps. 51:1–17).

God did not "despise" David's sincere confession; He accepted it. He saw David's broken heart, his contrite spirit, and He forgave him. But sow serious sin and you will reap serious consequences.

God can take something so wrong
and bring forth something beautiful.

The writer of Second Samuel goes on in chapter 12 to catalog the consequences David would suffer because of his sin. One disaster after another. The death of their first child. Division in the family. Rape. Murder. Revolt. The king would spend the rest of his life regretting this moral failure, yet praising the God who could take something so wrong and bring forth something beautiful.

It's Never Too Late

Perhaps you have been involved with someone sexually who is not your "one-flesh" partner. You now realize what a serious offense sexual sin is to God and you wonder if He could ever forgive you. It could be that having read this book, you're afraid you've blown your chance at the King's Feast. Will He ever invite you to the table again?

The truth about sexuality can be painful, but pain is not always bad. My mom suffers from eye problems that could potentially destroy her vision. Her great frustration is that there are no obvious symptoms. There is no pain. The pressure in her eyes could be extremely high and dangerous, but she has no way of knowing apart from regular eye exams. A little pain would be a helpful warning sign.

Pain is one way your body warns you of impending health problems. The same is true of spiritual pain. If you can sin and not feel pain and conviction, you are in danger of self-destruction. If you are feeling the conviction and pain of your sexual sin, be thankful. God is at work in your life. It's those who no longer feel anything who are in serious trouble.

Can you be restored and walk in purity again? Yes, thank God, you can. God's grace is a wonderful thing. In answer to sincere confession, He will reach down in love and compassion, like the gardener in the parable, and give you a fresh start. "If we confess our sins, he is faithful and just and will forgive us our sins and purify us from all unrighteousness" (1 John 1:9).

To confess sin means to "agree with God." You must agree that what you have done is evil before a holy God. When you take this step, you have God's assurance that He will meet you there. He will forgive your sin and purify you of all unrighteousness.

How much sin does He forgive? How much unrighteousness is covered? Read it for yourself: The Word says "*all* unrighteousness." And that's a promise.

You can't change the past. You cannot go back and undo what has been done. But you can decide to live differently from this day forward. Recognizing your sin and confessing it is good and necessary. Wallowing in your past sin is destructive and accomplishes nothing.

It is never too late to commit to sexual purity.

You may want to write this down on 3 x 5 cards and carry them with you, or tape them on your bathroom mirror or on the fridge. These words can change your life: IT IS NEVER TOO LATE TO BEGIN AGAIN. IT IS NEVER TOO LATE FOR GOD'S FORGIVENESS. IT IS NEVER TOO LATE TO COMMIT TO SEXUAL PURITY. SEXUAL SIN IS NOT AN UNPARDONABLE SIN.

God's greatest desire for you today is to confess your sin and determine, with His help, to live a life of purity. Believe it! Receive it! Then do it!

Chapter 15
The Road to Paradise

Life is a journey, a series of steps and choices, leading to an ultimate destination. For forgiven sinners, that destination is heaven. Someday we're going to live with God in a place that will eclipse Adam and Eve's garden paradise. No more temptation. No more tests. No more tears. Only joy forevermore.

Forgiven people are called to take the high road, to witness to the world that there is something different about us, something they need for themselves. Like forgiveness. Like grace. Like mercy. It's up to us to introduce the world to Someone they ought to know—Someone who can correct their mistakes, forgive their sins, and lead them all the way Home, with no more detours.

When I was a student at the University of Nebraska, I needed transportation badly. Like so many college kids, I was on a tight budget. So I dropped by a used-car lot near the campus.

There she sat. Not a scratch or dent anywhere that I could see. Clean. Good tread on the tires. A little beauty. She was just a VW Beetle, but she looked good to me. And best of all, she was in my price range.

A very eager salesman was more than willing for me to take her out on a test drive. I got behind the wheel, he jumped into the passenger seat, and we took off.

We hadn't gone very far when I decided to try out the radio. Somehow, in adjusting the knobs, I started up the windshield wipers. There they were, scraping away, back and forth across the dry windshield with that sound that sets your teeth on edge. I fiddled with the knobs some more, but the wiper blades kept going.

Meanwhile the salesman hadn't said a word. I figured he was thinking, *This is just a green college kid. If I keep my mouth shut, maybe he won't notice.*

When I turned the next corner, the horn started honking. Oh, great! Now the wipers are wiping and the horn is blowing. What next?

"Hit the steering wheel," the salesman suggested. I proceeded to follow directions. When that didn't bring about the desired results, my traveling companion tried to help by banging on the dashboard. All he succeeded in doing was knocking the flimsy dash off onto the front seat.

With the horn still blaring, wipers swiping, and the dashboard in our laps, we limped back to the car lot, where I breathed a sigh of relief and switched off the ignition.

The guy had not said another word—until now. With a bright, expectant look in his eye, he turned to me and said, "Well, what do you think?"

Needless to say, it was no deal.

Model Christians?

That used-car salesman was like a lot of Christians we know. The salesman wanted to pretend that the car was fine, even with all the evidence to the contrary. But what about us?

Lost people around us are shopping for something that will satisfy the longing in their souls. They want to know that what they see is what they will get, but they're clueless as to where to go for the truth. How can we convince them that Jesus is the answer?

As God's people, so often we live like the unbelieving world, then wonder why they don't want our Savior. If our behavior reflects the same sexual confusion others are experiencing, why should they want what we have? They've already tried that, and it didn't work. To be a witness to this world, we must be different, *other than* the world. The Bible calls this holiness. We must clearly demonstrate that holiness by the life we live, especially in matters of sexuality.

In our post-modern culture, people think with their feelings. They consider their experience to be a reliable measure of truth. As dangerous as this assumption is, you can use it to advantage. You can show others, by your own sexual contentment, that you have experienced the only Source of true satisfaction. You can model what it means to find pleasure in God. Believe me, in this empty and confused culture, people will notice. Your purity will shine like a lighthouse to those searching for help navigating the sexual fog of our times.

Purity Is a Process

In First Thessalonians 4, Paul has much to say about this journey we're on. "We urge and exhort in the Lord Jesus that you should abound more and more, just as you received from us how you ought to walk and to please God" (1 Thess. 4:1 NKJV). In this letter, originally written to the believers in Thessalonica, Paul recognizes that this life is a walk. Far from a stroll in the park, however, it an "advance," "a moving forward," "a progress toward." Learning to please God in our walk won't happen overnight. It will take a lifetime.

Maybe you hadn't thought about it this way, but you are not here on this earth primarily to please yourself—or even others. You are here to please God. To cause Him to delight in you as you glorify Him. To gladden His heart and bring him joy.

What gives God pleasure? John said it best when, inspired by the Holy Spirit, he echoed God's sentiments: "I have no greater joy than to hear that my children walk in truth" (3 John 4). Knowing that we are walking the walk—living up to the lessons we have learned from His written Word and His Spirit within us—actually gives our Father joy! He is delighted with us when we do well, when we pass the test, when we prove by our daily victories over temptation that we're "getting it."

We can't fake it. We have to be real. What we are in private is what we are. Regardless of the public debate in recent years, character does count. And it shows. While we're not perfect, only forgiven, what helps to keep us on track is to know that the world is watching. We owe it to them— and to the One who created us as sexual beings—not to let them down.

As we walk on in the forgiveness God has given us, we progress toward Christlikeness. To be like Christ is to be intimate with God, and to be intimate with God is pleasure forevermore. We cannot invite others to travel this path if we are not first willing to travel it ourselves.

Because He Said So

When Paul wrote First Thessalonians, he wasn't just making a suggestion or giving a recommendation. He wasn't listing the options. The subject—sexual purity—wasn't up for discussion. A lifetime of sexual purity was not his own idea; it was *God's* will (4:2).

I often get questions—have asked them myself—concerning how to know the will of God for our lives. Should I buy this house? Should I take this job? Should I marry this person?

Before we can find the answer to any of those questions, we have to ask ourselves another: Why do I want to know? Am I just looking for insider information so I won't make a bad decision? Our motives can be selfish. We ought to be asking for the purpose of bringing God glory, of pleasing Him.

Another good question is this: Am I being obedient to what God has already told me? I can hardly expect Him to reveal anything more until I am willing to do what He has shown me up to this point. For example, Paul told the Thessalonians (and us) that God's will for our walk is sexual purity. This means that before we start asking about career, money, spouse, or other important decisions, we'd better examine our sex lives. Is my behavior pure? Is my thought life free of contamination? What am I feeding my mind by what I watch on television or the Internet?

Paul was speaking to a society that was much like ours—rotten to the core. Sexual immorality was so rampant that some religions used temple prostitutes to engage "worshipers" in pagan rituals. The believers coming out of these heathen background sometimes carried this mind-set into Christianity. Paul was issuing a stern warning that these people were not to drift back into their old ways. Now that they were saved, it was time for a change. They were not supposed to look like, act like, or be like all the folks around them. They were to be different, distinct, set apart—sanctified.

Actually, even before Paul wrote his letter, some of these people knew better than they were doing. They had met Paul on an earlier visit to their city. He had spent time with them. He had taught them. They had seen him face to face.

Some of us know better too. We have met God through His Son, Jesus Christ. We know something about how He operates. Through the cycles of nature. Through our circumstances. Through prayer. Through the written Word. And now—as then—through the Holy Spirit. We have "seen" Him with our spiritual eyes. And someday we will see Him face to face.

For most of the decisions we make from day to day, the answers have already been given. Especially in the area of sexuality. It's a "simple" matter of obedience. Why would God tell us anything new if we're unwilling to obey what He has already told us?

What do we know? Let's retrace our steps one last time: We have discussed the theology of sexuality. Sex was created by God as a taste of the pleasure we can find in Him. We are to express our love, which is sourced in God, to a "one-flesh" partner in marriage. Sexuality is not a pursuit of something; rather, it is an expression of something. Sexuality is expressed in the context of relationship. As God designed it, your sexuality reflects His image.

When you relate to your "one-flesh" partner sexually, you are celebrating the image of God in you. In the process—when you "leave" and "cleave," becoming "one flesh"—you are afforded a beautiful picture of how God relates to Himself in the Trinity as three in one. Your sexuality also pictures that most precious and intimate relationship of God and His people, or Christ and His Church. That is the kind of intimacy God wants with you, His beloved.

The road to purity involves understanding the secret to sexual fulfillment, which is spiritual rather than physical. Only when you are right with God and intimate with Him are you able to put your sexuality in its proper place in your life.

If you are married, even your "one-flesh" partner can't fully satisfy apart from God. The sexual relationship is only a taste of the intimacy that ultimately satisfies: intimacy with God. Those who are still single must remember that their sexual drive is the soul's longing to be intimate with God. Rather than stuffing your passions, simply rechannel them to the One who can satisfy them.

If you have been involved in sexual sin, there is both bad news and good news. The bad news is that there are deeper scars left by this kind of sin than any other. The good news is that God's all-encompassing grace and mercy are available. He stands ready and willing to forgive and restore if you will confess and ask.

The road back may be hard, but there is a way. *Jesus* is that Way. If you want to be sure you never get lost again, follow Him. Do what He says to do . . . because He said so.

Passionate People

There is nothing wrong with passion. God wired us to be passionate people. It all depends, however, on one's purpose and motivation. Paul warns us of the dangers of lustful passions (1 Thess. 4:5). Lustful passions are those that control people and lead them into a pattern of sin in which they become slaves to their animal appetites. Made in the image of God, they are driven by natural instinct, like unreasoning animals. That, of course, is the pathway to destruction.

Lustful passion is what causes a person to throw away a marriage for some fling that can't last. It explains why a person will risk disease and even death for a meaningless romp between the sheets. Why a father would fill his daughter's nights with terror, then hate himself in the morning. Lust is a cruel taskmaster.

But passion is not always X-rated. Passion also implies "an intense, driving conviction" or "energetic and unflagging pursuit of an aim or devotion to a cause." Paul was passionate in his zeal to evangelize the lost and to father new believers in the faith. John was passionate in his love for his Mentor and Master, Jesus. Jesus is passionate about us. He calls us His friends, His beloved, His bride.

God did not make us passionate people to destroy us. Passion, focused in the right direction, allows us to experience a deeper and more meaningful relationship with God. It allows us to hear His heartbeat, to feel His love, to see with His eyes, to enjoy His presence, to savor all the joys of the world He has created. The more passionate our relationship with God, the more we have to offer our "one-flesh" partner. Or, for the unmarried, the more energy and devotion we have to offer a needy world.

We cannot walk this walk on our own. We cannot be what God called us to be apart from the power of God working in us. We cannot fulfill His will of sexual purity—either abstinence or commitment to our "one-flesh" partner—by ourselves.

Yet sexual purity is not an impossible dream. God has not left us powerless, doomed to fail. He has given every believer His Spirit to be our Helper, our Enabler, our Companion on the journey. It is the Spirit who makes it possible for us to do what God has called us to do, what He has called us to be. We are forgiven, fueled by His power, and set free . . . .

Free Indeed!

Imagine that you and I are in a footrace. As competitors, we are evenly matched. We are about the same weight and build and are in good physical condition. We run at about the same speed.

Also imagine that both of us have been asked to pull a fifty-pound sack tied around one ankle. At the last minute, one of the officials steps forward and cuts the cord from your sack, freeing you to run unencumbered. Got any doubt as to who would win the race?

As believers who have been set free from the weight of our sin, we are Olympic material. Our performance should be radically different from those who are still chained to old habits and lifestyles. The world is watching. How are you doing? Are you walking in the freedom God has released in you? Or are you still succumbing to temptation?

God is looking for winners. There is no shortage of Christians who have run the race poorly. Moral failure is even rampant among leaders in the Church. People don't believe our message because they don't see consistent evidence of God's power in our lives. Gandhi once said, "Show me redeemed lives and I might be inclined to believe in your Redeemer." Fair enough.

God is looking for winners and witnesses, people who are willing to model the successful Christian life. He is recruiting those who will discipline their minds, their emotions, and their bodies, channeling their passions in the right direction and running to win.

What do you say? Won't you choose to be a winner? To cross the finish line and show others how it's done?

Parable of
the Golden Goblets

✝

Parable of the Golden Goblets

He was a poor man, a cobbler by trade. The village business put food on the table, but that was about all, and only a few scraps of bread at that. He seemed happy enough in his meager surroundings, but times were hard.

His two beautiful little girls were the pride of his life. He would not have traded a pot of gold a thousand times over for the joy his twin daughters brought him. They were just children, but he was convinced that they were the brightest children in the village. Perhaps he was right. Then again, perhaps not.

The mother of the twins had died shortly after their birth. A part of the poor cobbler died that day with his dear wife, but another part came to life in his daughters. They were the last gift his wife had given him, and he would cherish them always.

It broke his heart that he could not give his sweet darlings everything the other children had. His girls deserved better, but all he could give them was his love. On occasion, he would even go without food to save a few coins to buy them some special treat. He was always thinking of ways to improve their lot and to demonstrate his love.

It was his loving heart that led the poor cobbler to do something quite unusual . . . .

✝

As he made preparations for the evening, he was so excited he was almost giddy. When everything was ready, he invited the girls to sit down at a table he had made festive with a branch of cherry blossoms arranged in a cracked vase.

"What is it, Father?" asked one daughter, quite puzzled.

"Yes, do tell us why we are celebrating!" said the other.

"Not until after supper," the old cobbler said, suppressing a smile. The meal, more abundant than usual, was tasty, and the conversation, a delight. They laughed and sang like children.

After the food was cleared from the table, the poor cobbler placed a box in front of each of his daughters. "But it's not our birthday! What could this be?" they asked in unison.

"Something special for each of you," he replied.

The girls tore open their packages. Inside were matching goblets that appeared to be made of pure gold. "It's . . . lovely!" gasped one of the daughters. The other hesitated, then halfheartedly agreed. The goblets sparkled and shone, reflecting the candlelight, as the girls held them up to admire them.

"But, Father," began the first daughter, "why did you do such a thing? How could you afford anything so grand?"

"I cannot always be with you," the cobbler answered. "These golden goblets will remind you that you are my priceless treasures, of great worth and value to me, and that I love you." A frown creased the brow of the other daughter. "But . . . how did you pay for them, Father?"

A tear glimmered in the poor cobbler's eye. "That is my concern, little one. Yours is to treasure the goblet. To keep it with you always. Soon I must go away, and you will marry. Never forget what we have had together." With that the poor cobbler left the room to gather his composure.

The first daughter continued to ponder. "How could Father afford such a rich gift for us?" she asked her sister.

"Don't be silly! These are not real golden goblets, of course. We will always be poor cobbler's daughters. Father only hoped we wouldn't notice that they are nothing but junk." With that, the second sister set her goblet aside and went about the business of clearing away the remains of the supper.

Soon afterward, the cobbler did, indeed, leave home, but his daughters never married. They missed their father and often wondered where he had gone. They received letters from him on occasion, but they never saw him again. In time, the letters stopped coming.

On a fine spring morning, word came to the village that the king would be passing through the village on a visit across his kingdom. He was a good king, who had assumed the throne after his wicked older brother was drowned at sea. The subjects had suffered under the harsh rule of the wicked brother, but now enjoyed prosperity and freedom under the new monarch.

A royal visit was a rare event, and it was customary for each of the villagers to give the king a gift. "But what shall we give him?" one of the twins moaned. "We have nothing of value—at least, nothing fine enough for a king."

"Oh, but we have!" said the other, going to retrieve the gift their father had given them. "I will give the king my golden goblet. It is my most prized possession."

"Oh, that old thing? Hmph! It's only junk," scoffed her sister. "Good for nothing but digging potatoes in the garden."

On the day of the king's visit, the streets, decorated for the gala event, were lined with villagers. Each of them had brought their treasures. He accepted them graciously, as was his nature.

One of the sisters stayed well back of the crowd since she had nothing of value for the king. Then, to her surprise and embarrassment, her twin stepped forward, holding the golden goblet. "This is my dearest treasure in all the world," she said to the king as she placed it at his feet. "I want you to have it."

The king stared at her, bemused. He picked up the goblet, turned it this way and that, but was unable to speak for some time. At last he found his voice. "Where did you get this?" he asked in a choked tone.

"It was a gift from my father," she replied. "He gave one to me and one to my sister to remind us of his love for us. He told us that we are his true treasures."

"Could it be . . . ," the king began, more to himself than to her, it seemed, "that you are the daughter of the cobbler?"

The poor girl nearly collapsed in shock. "Yes, my father is a cobbler. But how could you know? He has been away for many years."

The king's smile was tinged with bitterness. "Your father purchased these golden goblets from my brother, the wicked king. Since the cobbler had no money, he sold himself in exchange for the goblets. Your father became a slave to my brother, with time only to deliver these gifts and say his farewells. He spent the rest of his life as a faithful but mistreated slave."

The girl stood staring in amazement, tears flowing down her cheeks.

"When I became king," he said kindly, "I met your father and learned of his plight. I planned to give him his freedom so that he could return to his family . . . but he died before arrangements could be made." He paused, then cleared his throat. "He gave his life so that you might have this fine goblet—a treasure of incomparable value in this, or any, kingdom."

Hearing this, the other sister stood stunned and silent in the crowd. So the goblets were pure gold, after all.

Then the king spoke again. "There were two goblets and two daughters. Where is the other one?"

The crowd parted, and the second sister crept forward, her head low.

"Go quickly," he ordered her. "Bring the other goblet. I want to see them both."

She froze on the spot, wishing she could crawl into a crack in the cobblestone street. What was she supposed to do now? The other goblet was ruined, tarnished and covered with dirt. But perhaps if she polished it.....

She did as she was told and rushed home to look for the goblet, which must be somewhere outside, near the garden. But when she found it, try as she might, she could not remove the horrid stains.

The careless daughter tried to hide her goblet from the crowd as she carried it to the king, but she could hear their gasps of dismay. When the king saw the object, his face twisted. Whether in anger or in pity, it was hard to tell, but he stared at her for what seemed an eternity.

Then he put up his hand to quiet the murmurs of the crowd. "Was your father's love so meaningless to you that you neglected his gift?"

"I thought it was worthless junk," she said with shame. "I knew my father was only a poor cobbler …."

The king held the stained goblet next to the shiny one and shook his head. Then, without another word, he turned his horse and rode off, taking the goblets with him.

One day without warning the king returned to the village and sent his emissaries to bring the twins before him. Both feared what lay ahead. One feared for herself; the other, for her sister.

When the first sister was presented to him, he handed her a shiny golden goblet. "Oh, no, your majesty!" she said, putting her hands behind her back and stepping away. "You must be mistaken. That's not mine. I spoiled my goblet. This is the one my sister cherished."

"Ah, you are wrong, my dear young lady. Here is your sister's goblet." Turning to his squire, he waited while the man produced another sparkling golden goblet from a knapsack. "The other one is indeed yours. I took it back to the castle and had it restored. It looks like new again, with only a trace of its ill treatment."

"But I don't understand . . . why?"

"Because a treasure is always a treasure, whether it is treated as one or not. This goblet is too valuable to discard. I have restored it and am entrusting it again to your care. Will you guard it well this time?"

"Yes! Yes!" she replied, clasping the golden vessel to her. "I will never again doubt its value. What the king treasures, I will treasure!"

"So be it," said the king as he rode away.

From that day forward, the second daughter never again questioned her father's love. He had given them both priceless treasures—one, a little more scarred than the other, to be sure. But you would have to know the story to notice.

As we come to the end of the road, my prayer for you is that you will savor the King's Feast rather than settle for scraps. That you will be shaped by the image of the Father. That you will allow the Master to control the strings of your life. That you will bloom under the tender care of the Gardener of our souls. That you will prize and preserve the golden chalice of your sexuality so you may present yourself to the King, untarnished. That you will truly experience all it's meant to be!